A COMPLETE INTRODUCTION TO

CORYDORAS

and Related Catfishes

CO-015

Corydoras catfishes and kids go together—chances are that young children will see more of *Corydoras* species than most other fishes in a community aquarium, because the corys stay mostly at the bottom of the tank, more or less on a level with young children's eyes. Photo by Dr. Herbert R. Axelrod.

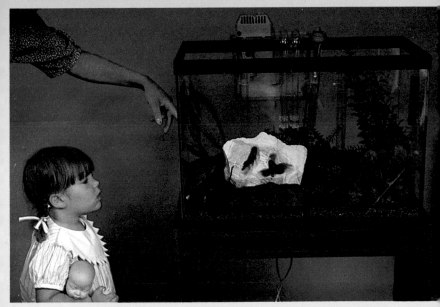

Corydoras paleatus is one of the most commonly available species for home aquaria. Here a pair is seen head on. Photo: H.-J. Richter.

A COMPLETE INTRODUCTION TO

CORYDORAS

and Related Catfishes

Corydoras metae. *Photo: Dr. Herbert R. Axelrod.*

A COMPLETE INTRODUCTION TO

CORYDORAS

and Related Catfishes

COMPLETELY ILLUSTRATED IN FULL-COLOR

Dr. Warren E. Burgess

Distributed in the UNITED STATES by T.F.H. Publications, Inc., 211 West Sylvania Avenue, Neptune City, NJ 07753; in CANADA to the Pet Trade by H & L Pet Supplies Inc., 27 Kingston Crescent, Kitchener, Ontario N2B 2T6; Rolf C. Hagen Ltd., 3225 Sartelon Street, Montreal 382 Quebec; in CANADA to the Book Trade by Macmillan of Canada (A Division of Canada Publishing Corporation), 164 Commander Boulevard, Agincourt, Ontario M1S 3C7; in ENGLAND by T.F.H. Publications Limited, 4 Kier Park, Ascot, Berkshire SL5 7DS; in AUSTRALIA AND THE SOUTH PACIFIC by T.F.H. (Australia) Pty. Ltd., Box 149, Brookvale 2100 N.S.W., Australia; in NEW ZEALAND by Ross Haines & Son, Ltd., 18 Monmouth Street, Grey Lynn, Auckland 2 New Zealand; in SINGAPORE AND MALAYSIA by MPH Distributors (S) Pte., Ltd., 601 Sims Drive, #03/07/21, Singapore 1438; in the PHILIPPINES by Bio-Research, 5 Lippay Street, San Lorenzo Village, Makati Rizal; in SOUTH AFRICA by Multipet Pty. Ltd., 30 Turners Avenue, Durban 4001. Published by T.F.H. Publications Inc. Manufactured in the United States of America by T.F.H. Publications, Inc.

Contents

Preface

Catfishes in the Aquarium

Why the name *catfishes*? Probably because of the association in some peoples' minds of the whiskers of the true cats (felines) and the barbels of the fishes. Most scientists agree that these barbels are sensory organs that help the catfishes locate food by probing around the bottom, where they are usually found. Often this is when the light level is low, for many catfishes are nocturnal, preferring to hide during the daytime, as they are obviously uncomfortable in bright light.

Because of their feeding habits, grubbing around the aquarium bottom searching for food, catfishes have become the "scavengers" of the aquarium and hobbyists look to them to help clean up uneaten food particles that fall to the bottom. Unfortunately many aquarists rely on these scraps to keep their catfishes well fed, not providing them with the same proper diet that they would for the other "more important" members of the community tank. But these catfishes are adaptable and some even learn to seek food at the surface, where they often turn upside down, feeding as if the surface were actually the bottom. Catfishes should be given a proper diet, making sure they receive as much nutritious food as the other fishes.

For the clean-up job, the most

reliable species (and among the most variable as well) belong to the armored catfishes, family Callichthyidae. They are armored in the sense that the body is covered with bony scutes or plates. Their inferior (directed toward the bottom) mouths are especially suited for bottom feeding, and the barbels are provided with sensory receptors for helping locate and recognize potential food items. For the beginning catfish lover, and those who keep them only casually as scavengers, the callichthyids (*Corydoras* and their relatives) are the perfect catfishes. They are readily available (over 100 species have been described), generally very inexpensive,

peaceful (they will not bedevil the other fishes in the tank very much), and even spawnable, a feature not often encountered among the catfishes.

Other catfishes, like the very popular *Synodontis* species from Africa, will be treated in my more extensive book *CATFISHES OF THE WORLD*.

From foreground to background: Corydoras trilineatus, C. ambiacus, *and* C. melanistius. *Photo: Dr. Herbert R. Axelrod.*

Introduction

The family Callichthyidae is a large family of relatively small, heavily armored freshwater catfishes from South America and Trinidad. Most are bottom-dwelling fishes, and they occur in a variety of habitats from slow-flowing streams and drainage ditches to ponds and even flooded areas. Some are able to live in swampy or muddy areas where the oxygen has become depleted. They can do this by virtue of their ability to take atmospheric air into the mouth and pass it on to their intestines where the oxygen is extracted. In humid areas or during rains many species are able to travel out of the water over land obstacles such as sand banks or mud flats to find food or better conditions. Most of the species live in large schools (often composed of mixed species) in sandy or weedy areas or as smaller groups in the slow-flowing streams. The natural diet of most species consists of worms and insect larvae that they root out with the use of their barbels in the soft sandy or muddy bottom material. Although relatively small, the larger, more abundant species are utilized as food by man. These are roasted in their armor and when done broken apart to obtain the flesh. Although this is easily accomplished with the *Corydoras* species, with *Callichthys* the use of a stone or other implement is needed to break through the armor.

In aquaria callichthyids are adaptable to a wide variety of conditions and as such are probably the most used of any of the catfish families in a community tank. They are peaceful and their armor enables them to survive attacks by all but the most aggressive fishes (usually cichlids). This armor also helps prevent parasitic attacks and, if accidents should happen where the catfish is out of water for a time (jumping out of a broken tank), prevents them from drying out very quickly. The tank size can vary considerably depending upon the size and activity of the species. For the

Habitat at Humaita, Brazil, where two species of large Corydoras *were captured. Photo: Dr. Herbert R. Axelrod.*

large bubblenest builders a 20-gallon tank or larger is necessary; for some of the dwarf corys even a 5-gallon tank will suffice if not too crowded. The bottom material has been argued about for many years. Some aquarists believe no bottom material should be used. Others say only soft material can be used because of the erosive effects of large, sharp gravel withstand a temperature range of about 8° to 36°C (also dependent upon the species), they should be kept within the range of 18° to 32°C. Normal filtration and some aeration (especially for the bubblenest builders) should be used. The diet should be varied and sufficient. All too often these catfishes are placed in a tank solely to clean up after the *real*

Live tubificid worms are one of the best live foods for catfishes. They can be restricted in the tank by using shallow dishes as seen here. Photo: Dr. Herbert R. Axelrod.

pieces on the delicate barbels. Actually, almost any bottom material can be used except those that do have very sharp edges (even this might be all right, but why take any chances). Normal planting and rockwork should be added, the lighting can be normal (these fishes are mostly diurnal), and the water should be close to neutral or slightly on the alkaline side (this varies with the species) and soft. Some aquarists advocate up to three tablespoons of salt per four gallons of water, but this is not necessary and not recommended unless other inhabitants of the community tank need it. Although callichthyids can in general

fishes and may not get enough food. They will accept almost anything, although live foods such as tubificid worms and other live foods that will sink to the bottom are best. Flake foods and other slow-sinking materials should be added in sufficient quantity to reach the bottom if there are fast-swimming mid- or upper-layer feeders in the tank. More specific information, including breeding techniques, will be given under the individual species.

Callichthyids have their entire flanks covered by only two lateral rows of bony dermal scutes. These are arranged so that they overlap along the rows as well as

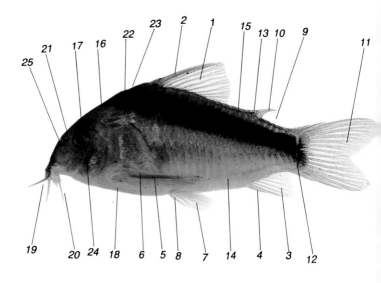

Schematic diagram of a generalized Corydoras *species.*
1. Dorsal Fin. 2. Dorsal Fin Spine. 3. Anal Fin. 4. Anal Fin Spine. 5. Pectoral Fin. 6. Pectoral Fin Spine. 7. Ventral Fin. 8. Ventral Fin Spine. 9. Adipose Fin. 10. Adipose Fin Spine. 11. Caudal Fin. 12. Caudal Peduncle. 13. Preadipose scutes. 14. Ventro-lateral Scutes. 15. Supra-lateral Scutes. 16. Supraoccipital. 17. Interorbital Area. 18. Coracoid Region. 19. Mental Barbel. 20. Rictal Barbels. 21. Nasal Opening. 22. Lateral Line Canal. 23. Nuchal Scutes. 24. Suborbital. 25. Snout.

between the rows, giving full protection but at the same time allowing a certain freedom of movement. Anteriorly these scutes connect with the solid bones of the head, and the head itself may be covered with bony plates. The upper row of lateral scutes may either meet on the back or there may be a narrow bare area that may or may not be filled in with small oval or roundish bony platelets. The body is usually rather deep and the upper profile of the head is steep. The eyes are usually large and movable, a condition that has caused some aquarists to swear that these little catfishes were actually winking at them. Actually the winking that they see is only an illusion caused by the movement of the eyes. There are two pairs of well-developed barbels and a pair of thread-like processes on the upper jaw, and a pair of fleshy flaps or one or two pairs of fleshy flaps or a pair of "barbels" on the underlip. The simplest arrangement of barbels is in *Hoplosternum* and *Callichthys,* with two pairs of well-developed barbels and a pair of thread-like processes on the

Photo of the actual barbels of two individuals of Corydoras aeneus.

upper jaw and a pair of fleshy flaps on the lower. In *Dianema* and *Cataphractops* the arrangement is similar but the lower lip has two pairs of fleshy barbel-like flaps. In *Aspidoras, Corydoras,* and *Brochis* the lower lip flaps are more developed and barbel-like and there are no thread-like appendages on the upper lip. The mouth is small and inferior. The large dorsal fin has a strong spine, as do the pectoral fins, both of which can be locked into a fully extended position. An adipose fin is present and consists of a stout, movable spine followed by a flap of skin. The swim bladder is short and two-chambered and is encased in bone. Some of the scutes or bony plates and fin spines may be covered with hair-like denticles; these are more developed on the head and fin spines of some males of some genera.

Seven genera are currently accepted as valid *(Cascadura* is said to be a young form of *Hoplosternum)* and can be distinguished by the following key (after Gosline, 1940):

15

1a. Snout depressed; interorbital width greater than or equal to head depth at anterior margin of orbit .... Subfamily Callichthyinae.....2

1b. Snout compressed or rounded; interorbital width considerably less than head depth at anterior margin of orbit; rictal barbels short, not reaching much beyond gill opening; lower lip reverted to form single pair of short barbels.................................... Subfamily Corydoradinae.....5

2a. Eyes more or less superior, the diameter contained two or more times in their distance from lower end of bony opercle 3

2b. Eyes lateral, the diameter contained 1.3 times or less in distance from lower end of bony opercle 4

3a. Coracoids expanded on abdominal surface between pectoral fin bases; suborbital bones not covered with flesh ....*Hoplosternum*

3b. Abdomen between pectoral fin bases completely covered with flesh; suborbitals

The tiny, more or less superior positioned eyes and the fleshy suborbitals help identify this species as Callichthys callichthys. *Photo: H. Hansen.*

Most of the more than one hundred Corydoras *species look very much alike. This one is* Corydoras axelrodi, *named for Dr. Herbert R. Axelrod. Photo: Dr. Herbert R. Axelrod.*

covered with flesh ....
....*Callichthys*

4a. Nuchal scutes not meeting
dorsally ....*Cataphractops*

4b. Nuchal scutes fused across
midline between occipital and
dorsal................. .....*Dianema*

5a. Nuchal scutes not meeting
above; coracoids more or
less expanded; frontal
fontanel elongate; no
supraoccipital fontanel.........6

5b. Nuchal scutes meeting or not
along midline between
occipital and dorsal;
abdomen between pectoral
fin bases entirely covered
with flesh; two cranial
fontanels present, a
supraoccipital fontanel and a
small roundish or elongate
frontal fontanel. .....*Aspidoras*

6a. D. I,7-9............... .....*Corydoras*

6b. D. I,10-18...................*Brochis*

Callichthyinae

Probably the most popular member of the subfamily Callichthyinae is this Dianema urostriatum. *The supposedly unique color pattern of the caudal fin was recently also discovered in a species of* Corydoras. *Photo Dr. Herbert R. Axelrod.*

The family Callichthyidae is generally divided into two subfamilies, Callichthyinae and Corydoradinae, that can be distinguished by the characters given in the above key. The subfamily Callichthyinae is said to be the more primitive of the two and includes the genera *Hoplosternum, Callichthys, Dianema,* and *Cataphractops.*

Hoedeman prefers to further divide the subfamily into two tribes, with *Dianema* and *Cataphractops* in the Dianemini, and *Hoplosternum* and *Callichthys* in the Callichthyini. The genus *Cascadura* was found to be only a young *Hoplosternum* in which the body scutes were not yet fully developed. (*Callichthys* has been separated

18

into its own subfamily by Miranda-Ribeiro (1959), the other genera *(Hoplosternum, Cataphractops,* and *Dianema)* being place by him in the subfamily Hoplosterninae).

Callichthys and *Hoplosternum* are normally found on the muddy bottoms of slow-flowing rivers, pools, drainage ditches, and swampy areas. In these latter areas they are capable of utilizing atmospheric air by taking in a gulp of air at the surface of the water and passing it back to the hind gut. The walls of the gut are lined with a mesh of tiny blood vessels into which the oxygen from the air can pass much as in true lungs. The number of trips a particular individual makes to the surface appears to be dependent upon the amount of oxygen in the water: less oxygen means more trips to the surface. The remaining gases pass out through the anus. When there is a severe drought the air breathers are, of course, the last to die, although when things get too bad these catfishes are able to traverse short stretches of land seeking better conditions. One *Hoplosternum* was observed to travel about 90 meters in the course of two hours. Both genera are commonly found in large schools and are easily netted, although removing them from a net is often a very long and arduous task for the spines catch in the meshwork and are difficult to disentangle. In some cases these fishes can be caught by hand, making things a bit easier. These catfishes are also capable of making sounds, both grunts and squeaks.

Spawning has been accomplished for both genera in aquaria. Both build bubblenests constructed from plant parts, some bottom material, and bubbles (formed by a mouth secretion and air). Additional bubbles are blown into the bottom portion of the nest until an almost solid mass about 20 cm in diameter and up to 10 cm high is formed. In most cases the male is the one that builds the nest. He is said to utilize his toothed pectoral spines in cutting off bits of plants and his barbels for setting them into the proper position. During the construction of the nest the female is either completely ignored or actively chased away. When the nest construction is finished the male will finally accept the female. The female will expel several eggs into a basket formed by the folding together of her ventral fins. These

When nestbuilding is virtually completed, the male will seek out a plump female. Usually there are some nearby that have already been attracted by the activity of the male. Photo: R. Zukal.

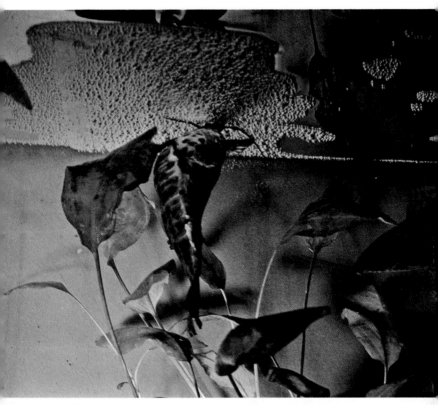

The female will expel several eggs into her ventral fin basket and carry them to the bubblenest. She will then invert and deposit them in the nest. Photo: B. Biegner.

are carried to the nest, and as she flips over on her back she deposits them among the bubbles. The male follows her and secures the eggs in place by adding more bubbles. There may eventually be several hundred eggs released by the female at one spawning. The male or the pair will keep watch over the nest for about four weeks. At that time the young catfishes, about 2.5 cm long, will come out of the nest. They are still vulnerable at that time for their armor is not yet fully hardened.

Feeding the fry and adults poses no problem. They will accept all normal aquarium foods. A substantial portion of vegetable matter should, however, be included.

CATAPHRACTOPS

The genus *Cataphractops* contains a single species from Peru and possibly Para. The body is compressed but the snout is depressed. The supraoccipital forms a short posterior projection that does not contact the azygous predorsal plate. The fontanel is elongate, and the nuchal plates do not fuse along the midline between the supraoccipital and the dorsal; the suborbital is naked. The coracoids are somewhat exposed on the abdomen between the pectoral fin bases. The eyes are large and lateral, visible as much from above as from below. The rictal barbels are long, extending as far as the end of the ventral fins or beyond that. The dorsal fin has a spine and 7 rays, its base shorter than the distance between it and the adipose fin. The caudal fin is emarginate.

DIANEMA

The genus *Dianema* contains only two species from the Amazon. The head is somewhat depressed, its width much less than the depth of the body. The fontanel is elongate, and the supraoccipital does not form a backward projection. The suborbital is very narrow and naked, and the nuchal plates fuse along the midline between the supraoccipital and the dorsal. The abdomen between the pectoral fin bases is usually completely covered by the expansion of the coracoids. There is no azygous predorsal plate. The eyes are large and lateral in position. The lower lip has two to four pairs of short barbel-like flaps in addition to the rictal barbels; the rictal barbels extend to the pectoral fin origin or beyond. The dorsal fin

A group of Dianema urostriatum *in a display tank. Food has apparently just been added as all the fish are searching over the bottom in characteristic fashion. Photo: Dr. Herbert R. Axelrod.*

Although a pair of Dianema urostriatum *will do well in a 10-gallon tank it is recommended that several be kept together in a small school in a larger aquarium of about 20 gallons.*

has a spine and 7 or 8 soft rays, its base length contained one to one and a half times in its distance from the adipose fin. The caudal fin is forked.

Species of the genus *Dianema* are commonly kept in home aquaria. A pair will do fairly well in a 10-gallon tank, but it is recommended that they be kept in small schools of about a dozen individuals, in which case a 20 to 30-gallon long tank is the smallest tank that should be considered. Filtration and aeration should be present and the tank should be well planted and some floating plants should

Dianema longibarbis *is less colorful than* urostriatum *and therefore less popular, but its care is essentially the same.*

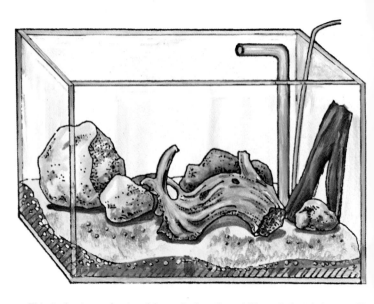

This is the type of setup (shown before the addition of plants) that could be made for callichthyid catfishes that are especially secretive, as it provides many places to hide; the placement of pieces of shale over the rocks to form caves would make the tank even more suitable for light-shy species.

be present. Sharp stones and sharp pieces of gravel should be avoided, and the tank itself must be covered. These fishes often swim in the middle parts of the tank and when startled (they are nervous fishes) are capable of easily leaping out of the tank. Luckily, they have the capability of aerial respiration and can survive for some time out of water in a wet or damp atmosphere. In fact, in their natural habitat they are reported to retreat into the mud and debris that is found along the bottom and sides of streams that have dried up, only to reappear during the next rainy season. Food is no problem as the list of foods accepted is very long and includes such items as worms of all types, insects and insect larvae, brine shrimp, daphnia, beefheart, frozen foods, and even flake foods. The optimum temperature range is 23° to 26°C.

According to various sources, sexes may be distinguished in several ways. The female, of course, is generally heavier than

the male. The soft portion of the pectoral fin of the male thickens into a creamy opaque pad; the female's pectoral membrane is transparent. A bubblenest is built, and the male's behavior is similar to that of the other bubblenest-building members of the subfamily. According to Langhammer, his pair built a huge bubblenest beneath a mat of water sprite. Another observer reported prespawning behavior in which the pair swam side by side as the female's belly took on a rosy hue and they investigated every centimeter of the tank. Unfortunately, there was no actual spawning.

Dianema longibarbis, the Porthole Catfish, is active and peaceful in aquaria. It stays in midwater most of the time, as does *D. urostriatum,* and may rest in an inclined position, head up, in the water column or against some support such as a plant leaf. This species attains a length of about 10 cm and is called the porthole catfish by virtue of a row of black dots along

Dianema urostriatum *is called the Flagtail Catfish because of the caudal fin pattern. Photo: K. Paysan.*

each side, although this is highly variable. The second species, *D. urostriatum,* is called the flagtail port because of the banded caudal fin, although this pattern may break up into a spotted pattern in older fish.

CALLICHTHYS

The genus *Callichthys* contains a single species. The head is broad and depressed, its width greater than the depth of the body; the body is compressed posteriorly. The fontanel is small, nearly circular, and the supraoccipital does not form a posterior extension. There is no azygous predorsal plate. The suborbital is covered with flesh and the nuchal plates fuse along the midline between the supraoccipital and the origin of the dorsal. The abdomen between the pectoral fins is completely covered with flesh.

Dianema longibarbis *is called the Porthole Catfish because of the row of dark spots extending from its eye to the caudal base.*

The eyes are small and superior in position while the nares are less than or equal to an orbit's diameter apart, the posterior one a diameter or less from the eye. The terminal mouth has the lower lip reverted to form a pair of fleshy flaps, and the premaxillary is rudimentary and without teeth; the lower jaw has an elongate patch of brown-tipped teeth on each side. The rictal barbels extend to midway between the pectoral and ventral fin bases. The dorsal fin has a flat spine and 7 or 8 rays, its base contained two or more times in its distance from the adipose fin. The anal fin is short and rounded and the caudal fin is broad and rounded. The ventral fins are rounded and inserted below the posterior half of the dorsal. The pectoral fin spine is short and thick, serrated on the inner margin in the young. The sides of the unpaired fins and the lower surface of the paired fins are thickly covered with short bristles; the opercle has a marginal group of short, slender bristles; and the posterior margins of the lateral plates have fine bristles. The gill openings are rather wide. Young individuals have a narrow band of teeth along the entire lower jaw, and the fontanel extends to the occipital and is divided near its middle. The lateral plates are not very deep and do not cover the entire sides. The nuchal plates are rudimentary.

Callichthys callichthys is very wide ranging, extending from Trinidad to Buenos Aires, and including the upper Amazon and Paraguay systems. They mostly inhabit fairly shallow still to slow-flowing waters with a muddy or fine material bottom and a dense growth of vegetation along the banks. They attain a length of about 20 cm in the wild but usually only about 14 cm in captivity. *Callichthys callichthys* is a peaceful and relatively

Planted with a variety of both rooted and floating plants, this aquarium provides a good deal of refuge for shy species. The gravel steeply banked in one corner would have a tendency to settle lower if continually picked over by grubbing Corydoras.

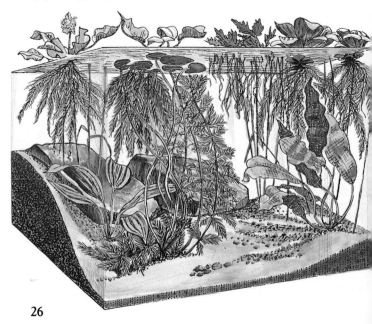

Equipped with a sponge filter and holding both a potted growing plant and a plant with heavy root structure, this tank would be suitable for the spawning of Callichthyid species exhibiting the Corydoras *spawning pattern. Drawing by* Andrew Prendimano.

undemanding species, usually active in dim light or at night but hiding when the light is bright. It is an excellent jumper and its tank should be well-covered. They need a large aquarium (at least a 20-gallon tank) although the water should be fairly shallow (about 13 cm or less), especially for breeding. Part of the reason for this is their habit of taking gulps of air from the surface from time to time which is eventually expelled at the anus. The bottom material should be fine and dark in color. Plants should be strong and well rooted; fine-leaved plants are not recommended as the bottom is constantly being stirred up and the fine leaves only seem to contribute to the mess. Surface plants, however, may be used for keeping the light level down and for breeding these

catfish. A temperature range of 24° to 26°C is adequate although for brief periods temperatures as low as 18°C can be tolerated. The water chemistry is not critical but the water should be kept clean. With such fishes that stir up the bottom, this means an efficient filtration system. *Callichthys callichthys* is easy to feed. It is what is known as an indiscriminate omnivore, meaning that it will accept almost anything, both animal and vegetable. This is an active and greedy feeder that prefers live foods but takes whiteworms, chopped earthworms, tubificid worms, bloodworms, frozen brine shrimp, beefheart mix, various salad items, etc. Although it is primarily a bottom forager, if it is not well fed it will include small fishes in its diet, probably taking them by surprise at night while they sleep. Being good scavengers they are accepted as community tank fishes even though they are shy and stir up the bottom regularly.

Spawning has been reported many times and, in fact, this species is being bred commercially, albeit not in large quantities. The females are larger and more robust, while the males are brighter in color, exhibiting a delicate blue or violet sheen laterally; the female is a rather dull olive-green. The males also have a more well developed and longer pectoral fin spine that is reddish brown and edged with orange or reddish orange. The plates cover the abdomen of the male fully but do not in the female; this gap is probably due to the expansion of the area as the female fills with eggs. For spawning this catfish, a large bare tank is commonly used, say about 20 gallons capacity. It is filled to about 25% capacity (no more than about 13 cm deep).

Some aquarists prefer to add some rocks or plants for hiding purposes. Floating on the surface should be a piece of styrofoam (or similar object) about 12 to 15 cm to a side or, for those who like the "natural" method, some floating plants such as water hyacinth. The water should be soft and warm (about 24°C) although some aquarists believe that 20°C is sufficient. The prospective parents should be conditioned with live foods and chopped earthworms and should be at least 10 cm in length. The pair (some aquarists prefer two or three males per female) can be added to the spawning tank in the evening with the expectation that the male will start construction of a bubblenest the following day. The males are aggressive at this time and when courting can be heard making quite audible grunts. If the action is a bit slow to start, the pair can be separated and further conditioned or a new combination tried. One spawner

Equipped with a sponge filter and a floating "nest" cover, this aquarium could be used as a spawning tank for nest-building callichthyids. Drawing by Andrew Prendimano.

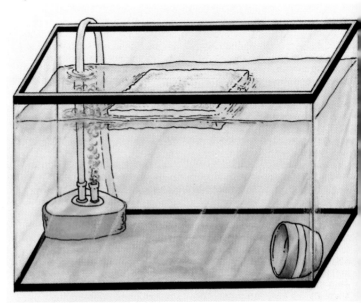

suggests that fluctuations in temperature may be an inducement for the onset of spawning.

If all goes well the male will start his bubblenest. In the wild this nest is constructed using clumps of overhanging grass, twigs, or floating plants; in the aquarium the floating plants or

and deposit about 15 to 20 eggs in it. The male will then "flip" her over on her back and with their ventral surfaces opposed he fertilizes the eggs. The female then swims to the bubblenest and deposits the eggs therein. The male may add more bubbles from time to time. This action is repeated again and again over

Callichthys callichthys *is a bubblenest builder that is being bred commercially, but not in great quantities. Photo: H.-J. Richter.*

styrofoam square will be utilized, or even a broad leaf of a bottom plant that has grown to the surface. The male will take in air from the surface in an inverted position and move to the undersurface of the nest site where he emits mucus-covered bubbles from his gill openings. This continues until a substantial bubblenest is completed (one was measured at 15 cm in diameter and some 6 cm in height). During nest construction the female is not allowed near the site although the male may nudge her abdomen from time to time between his bubble-making sessions.

Upon completion of the nest spawning will commence, usually in the morning. The female will form a pouch or basket by clamping her ventral fins together

the course of about two hours, when anywhere from 150 to 400 eggs are in the nest. The female is best removed after her eggs are depleted for both her protection (from the male) and the protection of the eggs (she may eat them). The male assumes the duty of guarding the nest full of eggs and does so with vigor. During this time he emits grunting noises, possibly as a warning. The fairly large (about 2 mm diameter) eggs are a transparent pink and should hatch in about four to five days. The fry apparently absorb the nourishment in the yolk sac during the incubation period and are free-swimming as soon as they hatch. The male can now be removed.

Within 24 hours the fry should receive rotifers, cyclops,

enchytrae, microworms, newly hatched brine shrimp, or even chopped tubificid worms. For best results feed at least three times a day. The fry and young grow rapidly at first but the growth rate slows down after a while. In a couple of months the young *Callichthys* should be at least 25 mm in length. The fry are a tan color sprinkled with black spots.

Although this species has been in the hobby for many, many years it has not attained the popularity of other species in the subfamily.

HOPLOSTERNUM

The genus *Hoplosternum* contains only three or four species (the fourth is still in question). The head is depressed, its width equal to or less than the width of the body.

The fontanel is rounded or elongate and the suborbital is naked. The supraoccipital does not form a posterior extension and there is no azygous predorsal plate. The nuchal plates fuse along the midline between the supraoccipital and the dorsal and the abdomen between the pectoral fins is totally or mostly enclosed by the expanded coracoids. The eyes are somewhat superiorly placed, being more visible from above than from below. The lower lip is reverted and forms a pair of fleshy flaps; the rictal barbels extend as far as midway between the pectoral and ventral fin bases or a bit farther. The dorsal fin has a spine and 7 or 8 rays, its base contained slightly more than one time in its distance from the adipose fin. The caudal fin may

The genus Hoplosternum *contains three to four species, all of which look quite similar. The head is depressed and the caudal peduncle is deep and compressed. This is* H. thoracatum.

be rounded or emarginate.

Hoplosternum littorale is distributed from Trinidad through Venezuela and the Guianas to the La Plata region. It is the largest of the *Hoplosternum* and *Callichthys* species, attaining a length of about 20 cm. It is common in marshes, swamps,

floating plants for protection from the light and for possible spawning action should be added. The water conditions are not critical but good filtration is a must. Water changes are beneficial, especially when combined with a siphoning of any bottom material that would be

One of the common patterns of Hoplosternum thoracatum. *This pattern is usually seen in younger fish. Photo: H.-J. Richter.*

and larger rivers where it feeds to a great extent on aquatic plants. In some areas it is fished for on a commercial basis as a food fish. It is not brightly colored, being a drab gray to grayish brown and only rarely with a few fine black spots. The caudal fin is forked. Aquarium care for this species is essentially the same as that for *Callichthys,* but it should have a temperature of about 24°C. Although not strictly nocturnal, *H. littorale* prefers subdued lighting. The smaller individuals are said to hide more than the larger ones. A large tank is recommended (20 gallons or more) suitably furnished with sand, rocks (without sharp edges), and coarse-leaved plants that are well rooted. Some

stirred up by these bottom dwellers. Food is also no problem as the hoplos will accept a wide variety of foods from live foods (which they prefer) to flake foods. They will even eat from the surface if sufficiently motivated by hunger.

The males have an enlarged, thickened pectoral fin spine that at maturity turns up at the end like a ski and with the onset of the spawning season takes on a maroon to blood-red coloration; in *H. thoracatum* the pectoral spine also becomes thickened but there are no reports of it turning up at the end and the color most quoted for it is orange, not dark red. Male *H. littorale* also have thickened and fused pectoral rays (the females less so) and the

Females usually have a gap between the coracoids, especially when they start filling up with eggs. The gap can plainly be seen in this Hoplosternum thoracatum. *Photo: K. Paysan.*

females usually have a gap in the pectoral region between the coracoids as they fill up with eggs. Like the other hoplos, this species is a bubblenest builder. As the temperature is raised slowly to about 26° or 27°C and possibly with the water change, the male will begin to construct his bubblenest and courtship begins. Surface material should be provided in the form of floating plants or a floating object such as a piece of styrofoam such as that used for *Callichthys*. If nothing is available the male will improvise by removing pieces of the rooted plants (possibly through use of his serrated pectoral fin spines by clamping them against the body with the leaf trapped inside) or by actually uprooting the plants themselves. The nest is fairly large, the diameter often exceeding 30 cm and the thickness 8 cm. The aeration should be kept at a low level so as not to disturb the nest.

After a complicated courtship ritual (unfortunately this was not described) about 200 to 300 (some report up to 500) amber eggs about 1 mm in diameter are placed in the nest. These are stuck together with a secretion similar to that which holds the nest bubbles together and another layer of bubbles is blown by the male under the eggs to hold them in the nest. The male stands guard over the nest after chasing the female from the vicinity. In about three to four days the fry hatch out and have already absorbed their yolk sac. They can be seen sticking to the plants and glass sides of the tank and are ready for food within 24 hours. Microworms and crushed flake food or similar fare can be used for the first few days and then larger food such as newly hatched brine shrimp should be added. The male can be removed once the eggs hatch. The fry grow quickly and before long are a dark gray with darker markings. However, they do not assume the bottom-dwelling habits of the adults until after about a couple of weeks. They develop their armor at a size of about 1.2 cm. In a year's time they should have grown to about 12.5 cm. Most of the spawnings reported for this species have occurred in the springtime, apparently coinciding with the onset of the rainy season in their natural habitat. It is

caudal base is crossed by a pale transverse band. The aquarium care is as given for *Callichthys*.

Of the larger callichthyids, *H. thoracatum* is said to be the easiest to spawn. The male's pectoral spine is thick and flattened and with the start of the spawning season turns a bright orange to orange-red. This species is ready to spawn at

Hoplosternum thoracatum *is one of the easier "hoplos" to spawn. A single male should be used as competition between males could lead to injury to one or both combatants. Photo: H.-J. Richter.*

suggested that the breeders not be spawned continuously but be allowed rest periods from time to time.

Hoplosternum thoracatum is a wide ranging species said to occur from southern Panama to Paraguay in a variety of different habitats. The color is quite variable, not only within a population but from one locality to another, but normally it is lighter than *Callichthys callichthys* and *H. littorale,* often being a rich reddish brown with dark spots (sometimes a few, sometimes numerous) on the upper part of the body and whitish spotted with black ventrally. The caudal fin is truncate and in both sexes the

about a year old when it has attained a size of 9 cm (fully grown it is 15-16 cm long), and spawns best in the springtime (April or May). Although not an aggressive species, males may become combative and actual damage can be done. Therefore only a single male should be used for spawning. A bubblenest is constructed by the male as in the other species, utilizing plant material if it is available. The water level should be relatively low, also similar to that for the other species. Courtship commences and eventually the male swims alongside the female. After some vibrations a "T" is formed, possibly with the male hanging vertically below the bubblenest. A batch of 10 to 30 eggs is deposited into the female's ventral basket and she swims upside down below the nest and deposits the eggs safely therein. She may at times sink to the bottom and rest between egg-laying bouts. There is a controversy as to when the eggs are fertilized by the male. Some say they are fertilized as soon as they are laid into the basket and while still in the "T" position; others say the eggs are deposited in the bubblenest and the male follows her there immediately to fertilize the eggs; still others report that the female takes sperm into her mouth while in the "T" position and, after sinking to the bottom and resting, she swims to the nest to deposit the eggs and fertilizes them herself with the sperm she has collected beforehand. The first two sound much more plausible than the last mainly because of the time involved before the eggs are fertilized in the last method. In any event the process continues until somewhat over 500 eggs are safely ensconced in the nest. The male drives off the female and guards the eggs.

The eggs hatch in four to five days but the fry may remain in the nest for several days afterward, apparently sheltering there until they are able to swim freely. Since the yolk in the yolk sac is virtually depleted upon hatching, the fry will be ready for food within 24 hours. Microworms and other similar sized live foods should be fed. Crushed flake food has also been given along with other foods with satisfactory results. Newly hatched brine shrimp can be added to the menu in a few days. When the young do become free-swimming they move to the bottom where they dig in and are very difficult to spot. They are dark in color and look like miniature adults. At this time they are very active and

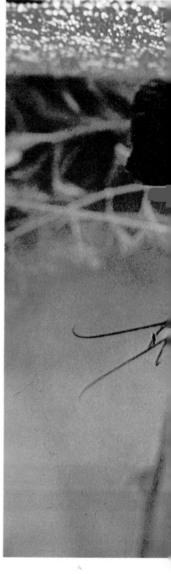

feedings should be sufficient and often.

Hoplosternum magdalenae is the questionable species. It is brownish gray with light yellowish white vertical barring of sorts along the sides. Some say this is one and the same with the "dwarf hoplo," a small species that is in the hobby but whose identity has (dubiously) been determined as

H. pectorale. The dwarf hoplo, as the name implies, is smaller than the other species, with a maximum length of some 12 cm. It is yellowish brown and covered with numerous small black spots. The caudal fin is forked and the tips are slightly rounded. This small active species can be housed in a smaller tank than the other two common hoplos, a 15-

After depositing a batch of eggs in the bubblenest, the female (note she is still plump with eggs) will nudge the male indicating she is ready for further action. Photo: R. Zukal.

gallon aquarium being okay for a half dozen or so individuals. Success has been achieved with a pH of 7.4, a temperature range of 22° to 26°C, and weekly partial water changes. As with the other hoplos, this fish is a good feeder and will accept a wide variety of aquarum foods, including even flake foods, but with live foods favored.

Sexes are distinguished by the relatively heavier pectoral spine of the male (the distinction is not so great as in the other hoplos). In addition, the dwarf hoplo has an opaque cream-colored nuptial pad in the soft rays of the pectoral fin of the male; the female's pectoral fin ray membranes remain transparent. The larger female also shows some smooth white skin between the coracoids as she fills up with eggs. Spawning has been accomplished/in a 7-gallon tank filled with about 5 gallons of water. There was no gravel, but a sponge filter, some floating plants, and a floating plastic lid were added. The temperature was 20-22°C. A pair was added

and the male built a bubblenest. A single male was used because competition for space and material develops with more than one male in a tank, and there are numerous encounters between the males. The male, when his nest is ready, will vigorously court the female, performing what has been referred to as a frenzied dance. The female extrudes some eggs and moves to the bubblenest to place them there; the male follows immediately and fertilizes them. After this act is repeated over a period of about 2 1/2 hours the female has exhausted her egg supply and is driven from the scene. She should be removed at this time.

Hatching at this temperature occurred in about a week and an additional three days were needed before the fry became free-swimming. Feeding should commence at this time. Several feedings per day are urged for best growth. Microworms, newly hatched brine shrimp, etc., are the most commonly used starter foods. Small water changes are recommended on a daily basis

One of the other species of Hoplosternum, H. pectorale. *Note the orange tint to the pectoral spine — possibly a male coming into spawning condition. Photo: Andre Roth.*

Most Hoplos are easily fed. Food that sinks to the bottom is best, but even floating flakes can be managed by hungry catfishes. Photo: B. Kahl.

for two weeks, then twice a week. At about six weeks the young hoplos can take chopped tubificid worms, chopped whiteworms, small daphnia, and still the baby brine. Crushed flake food may also be added.

It is interesting to note that reports on the other hoplos maintain the fry are free-swimming immediately upon hatching; in this species it is said that they remain in the nest for several days before becoming free-swimming. It could be possible that in the other species the actual hatching time was missed and that the time the fry left the nest was interpreted as hatching time.

Hoplosternum littorale is the largest of the hoplos, attaining a length of about 20 cm. It also prefers subdued lighting. Photo: Aaron Norman.

Corydoradinae

The subfamily Corydoradinae is said to be derived from *Hoplosternum*-like ancestors. It consists of three genera, *Aspidoras, Brochis,* and *Corydoras,* although the differences are not so great as to preclude some lumpers from considering them all in a single genus. Their biotope is similar to that of the Callichthyinae. All three genera have representatives in the aquarium hobby, but it is *Corydoras* that has gained the affection of almost every hobbyist and it is a rare sight to see a community tank without a few individuals scurrying about on the bottom searching for food. Most species are easy to care for, having no special demands as far as water chemistry is concerned as long as extremes are avoided. Since most species are bottom feeders and may stir the bottom up almost continuously, adequate filtration is required. Food type is no problem as almost anything edible is accepted. However, the aquarist must ensure that enough food reaches the bottom for the catfishes — not just leftovers but a well rounded diet. Live foods of

all kinds, especially worms, are recommended. A temperature range of about 18° to 26°C is generally adequate although some species have less of a range tolerance and need higher (or lower for cool water species) temperatures. In the wild many of the species inhabit slowly moving waters where they can be found in small groups to many hundreds in a single aggregation. The species may often be intermingled. They will investigate the bottom for food as well as the mud and sand banks or even leaves of aquatic or bog plants

Corydoras paleatus is one of the most commonly available species for home aquaria. Here a pair is seen head on. Photo: H.-J. Richter.

that can be reached. In an aquarium, members of some *Corydoras* species have been observed feeding upside down off the surface, so they do seem to be quite adaptable. Those species that live in swampy areas or places where their water supply might dwindle to next to nothing in the dry season are able to utilize their gut respiration mechanism to survive. It has been reported that thousands were found together, partly covered with wet mud, just surviving until the next rains. At the onset of the rains, they come to life and many start courting. Spawning in captivity has been achieved for members of all three genera. The various techniques are discussed under the appropriate genera and species.

ASPIDORAS

The genus *Aspidoras* is a moderately sized genus consisting of 14 species from Brazil. They are all small, the largest not surpassing 5 cm in length. The head is compressed and the supraoccipital forms a broad but short triangle posteriorly. There are two cranial fontanels. The anterior fontanel is small, roundish to elongate, its length equal to about half the eye diameter; the posterior or supraoccipital fontanel is closed in adult specimens, leaving only a small roundish shallow pit. The suborbital is naked and the nuchal plates barely meet along the midline between the supraoccipital and the azygous predorsal plate. The eyes are small and superior in position, and the abdomen between the pectoral fins is completely covered with flesh. The lower lip is reverted to form a single pair of barbels besides the rictal barbels, these latter extending as far as the gill opening. The dorsal has a spine and 7 rays, the dorsal fin base being somewhat shorter than its distance from the adipose fin; both dorsal and pectoral fin spines are short. The caudal fin is forked.

The character that serves to distinguish this genus from the others of the family is the number and shape of the cranial fontanels. Previous accounts relied on the position of the nuchal plates (meeting or not meeting) to distinguish between *Aspidoras* and *Corydoras*. However, this has proven to be inadequate, for in some species of *Aspidoras* they are separated along the midline by the

Species of Aspidoras *are quite small, the largest no more than 5 cm in length. This is* Aspidoras pauciradiatus. *Photo: Dr. Herbert R. Axelrod.*

Most species of Aspidoras *are similar and often hard to distinguish. Shown here is* Aspidoras lakoi. *Photo: Dr. Herbert R. Axelrod.*

supraoccipital process as in most (but not all) species of *Corydoras.* It was found that *Aspidoras* possessed two cranial fontanels, a supraoccipital fontanel and a small, roundish or oval to elongate frontal fontanel. In *Corydoras, Brochis,* and *Dianema* there is a single, open fontanel, albeit much larger and more elongate than that of *Aspidoras,* with a commisural bar anteriorly. *Callichthys* and *Hoplosternum* possess a rounded frontal fontanel with foramens both anterior and posterior to the commisural bar. In addition, except for *Aspidoras poecilus,* all

Aspidoras fuscoguttatus *or similar species. Without specimens it is often very difficult to positively identify a species. Photo: Dr. Herbert R. Axelrod.*

There is no question as to the identity of this fish. This is the actual holotype of Aspidoras pauciradiatus. *Photo: Dr. Herbert R. Axelrod.*

species of *Aspidoras* have a rounded transverse head shape as opposed to a triangularly depressed one.

Aspidoras do fairly well in aquaria under similar conditions as for most *Corydoras*. The water conditions that seem best are a pH of 6.8-7.0 and a temperature of about 22° to 26°C. The only species that seems to regularly appear in dealers' tanks is *Aspidoras pauciradiatus*. This little species has caused a bit of a stir as two separate populations are known, living contentedly a considerable distance apart, one in the Rio Negro and the other in the Rio Araguaia. The newer population was discovered nearly 3,000 river kilometers beyond the previously known range of the genus. The differences in the two populations (which will not be discussed here) are not clear enough to establish whether we are dealing with separate subspecies, separate species, or just normal variation for the species. Eggs were found in some of the female specimens of 16-23 mm SL (standard length).

In five male paratypes of *A. virgulatus* enlarged odontodes (bristles) such as are found in *Corydoras barbatus, C. macropterus, C. bondi coppenamensis,* and many species of Loricariidae were seen.

BROCHIS

The genus *Brochis* contains only three species, the most recent described in 1983. The body and head are compressed. The supraoccipital forms a projection extending along the midline to the azygous predorsal plate; the fontanel is elongate. The nuchal plates never meet along the mid-dorsal line and the coracoids are exposed ventrally between the pectoral fin bases. The eyes are more or less superior in position and the lower lip forms a single pair of short barbels in addition to the rictal barbels (a condition similar to that of the genus *Corydoras,* the unusual formations described by Cope due most likely to decay of the flesh behind the lips, as it was found to be in *Dianema*); the rictal barbels never extend much beyond the level of the gill openings. The dorsal fin has a spine and 10 to 18 rays, its base being much longer than its distance from the adipose fin; the caudal fin is forked.

Brochis is very similar to Corydoras but differs mainly in the deeper body and the higher number of dorsal fin rays, a character that can be used with confidence by aquarists. At first glance Brochis species appear like large Corydoras aeneus and, indeed, have many times been sold under that name. In fact, the behavior that both groups show is very much alike. Brochis are was actually Nijssen & Isbrücker (1970) who combined the two, giving sufficient reasons for doing so. B. splendens occurs in the upper reaches of the Amazon, Rio Ucayali to Pucallpa, Rio Ambiyacu, and the environs about Iquitos, where it is seen mostly in sluggish waters with dense vegetation along the banks. This species, which attains a length of between 7 and 9 cm, is called the emerald catfish or the emerald brochis because, depending upon the angle of the lighting, the body reflects a metallic green, a blue-green, or even a bluish color. The ventral area is yellow-ochre with

At first glance Brochis *species could be mistaken for* Corydoras *species but a look at the dorsal fin easily distinguishes them. This is* Brochis splendens, *the most commonly available species. Photo: B. Kahl.*

peaceful and hardy fishes that live in schools on the bottom. They are undemanding aquarium fishes that attain a length of about 8 cm.

Probably the most widely available species of Brochis in the aquarium trade is B. splendens. This species was once commonly called B. coeruleus. Gosline (1940) was the first to suspect the synonymy of coeruleus and splendens, but it the pectoral, ventral, and anal fins yellowish and the dorsal, caudal, and adipose fins a translucent brownish. This peaceful species is not very demanding and can be maintained under the same conditions as most Corydoras species. They are shy and easily frightened when kept as individuals so it is best to keep small groups (at least half a dozen or more). The tank (not under 80 liters) should have only soft, fine bottom material or if coarser material is desired it should be relegated to those parts of the tank where feeding does not occur. The aquarium should be thickly planted and decorated with driftwood, etc., so that sufficient hiding places are available. The water itself should be neutral (pH 7.0) and slightly hard with a temperature between 23° and 25°C. Strong filtration and a partial water change (preferably from the bottom) are essential. Feeding is not difficult. In the wild these bottom feeders dine on insect larvae, worms, and small crustaceans; in the aquarium almost anything is accepted although worms, especially tubificid worms, are preferred. *B. splendens* does well in a community tank, and does not tear up the plants.

Spawning has been accomplished for this species. Spawning, it has been suggested, is possibly a group affair, and success has been achieved with two females and three males on at least two occasions. It has also been suggested that it occurs on an annual basis, perhaps with the onset of the rainy season, for on one occasion the spawning took place as the barometer fell. The females are larger and more robust than the males and have a more pinkish belly as opposed to the more yellowish one of the male. The spawning tank is best without a substrate but supplied with a number of floating plants. The water should be soft (to 8° DH), slightly acid, and extremely clean. The temperature should be about 24° or 25°C. With the addition of three males and two females, all well conditioned on live foods, spawning should commence.

Essentially the spawning agrees very well with that of many *Corydoras* species, but differs as regards the details. First of all, *B. splendens* does not spawn in open water but on the

Brochis multiradiatus *as the name implies has more dorsal fin rays than* B. splendens. *Its snout is also more pointed.*

substrate. The female drops about ten eggs into her ventral fin basket and they are fertilized after some preliminary chasing. The eggs are then placed about the tank one by one until 300 eggs are scattered over the entire tank but with the floating surface plants *(Riccia fluitans* has been used) receiving the greatest share. The eggs, which are slightly larger than most cory eggs, are not bothered by the parents according to the reports.

The eggs hatch in approximately four days. After about two days the yolk sac is about depleted and newly hatched brine shrimp can be fed. After a few more days give finely chopped tubificid worms and microworms, grindal worms, and finely chopped enchytrae. The bottom should be siphoned frequently and daily water changes are strongly suggested starting with the feeding. At an age of about ten days the first color in the form of a darkish spot develops in the middle of the body. At two to three weeks of age the dorsal fin starts to become larger and is of a dark color. The emerald green color starts to develop at a size of about 35 mm when the young are some six weeks old. This starts as a number of spots that eventually coalesce. What is very striking is the development of the dorsal fin. In young individuals the dorsal fin is proportionally very large and it is very colorful, being orange with a variable pattern of dark markings. At an age of six months the young fish should be almost 5 cm in length.

Brochis multiradiatus has about 17 dorsal fin rays as compared with the 11 or 12 commonly seen in *B. splendens.* The snout is obviously longer than that of *splendens,* and for this reason the common name most usually applied to this species is Hog-nosed brochis. This species has either been quite rare in the hobby or has not been

Brochis splendens *undergoes some changes with growth as seen here. The juvenile (above) has a proportionately higher as well as more colorful dorsal fin than the adult (below). Photos: Dr. Warren E. Burgess (juv.); H.-J. Richter (adult).*

recognized—any many-rayed dorsal-finned cory-like catfish would naturally be referred to as *B. splendens,* especially since *multiradiatus* was at first known from a single specimen that was thought to be an aberrant *splendens.* The aquarium care is essentially the same as that for the emerald catfish.

The third species, *B. britskii,* also has a high number of dorsal fin rays (15-18). It has a shorter snout, a larger eye, grows to a larger size, and (uniquely in the family) has its head covered ventrally by a large shield extending beyond the tip of the mental barbels. It is not known if the young of this species have the large orange and black dorsal fin of the other two species.

CORYDORAS

The genus *Corydoras* is one of the two most important genera of catfishes as far as aquarists are concerned, the second being of course *Hypostomus* of the family Loricariidae. *Corydoras* is a very large genus with approximately 100 species, give or take a dozen depending upon the amount of variability allowed. They are almost all small forms ranging in size from 2.5 to about 12 cm with the majority in the range of 5 to 7 cm. The head and body are compressed, with the supraoccipital forming a process posteriorly that may or may not meet the azygous predorsal plate. The fontanel is elongate and the suborbital is naked. The sides of the body are covered by approximately 22 to 26 dorsolateral and 19 to 24 ventrolateral scutes. The number of azygous preadipose scutes and the number and position of small scutes on the caudal peduncle are variable, and the nuchal plates never meet along the mid-dorsal line. The area between the coracoid processes may or may not be covered by a mosaic of plates. The eyes are more or less superior in position. The lower lip has a single pair of short barbels in addition to the rictal barbels, these latter never reaching very much beyond the level of the gill openings. The dorsal fin has a spine and 7 (occasionally 8) rays, its base being equivalent to its distance from the adipose fin. The anal fin usually has i,6 and the ventral fin i,5 rays, whereas the pectoral fin has a spine and 8 rays. The number of pectoral fin rays and lateral body scutes may be higher in the so-called long-snouted species. The caudal fin is forked.

Nijssen (1970) attempted to break the large genus *Corydoras* down into species groups, a move that was again attempted in conjunction with Isbrücker in 1980. Although the first groups were somewhat defined on the basis of color pattern, snout length, etc., the second set of groups were only listed. The second set (of species described

Corydoras *species, like this* C. aeneus, *have shorter dorsal fins, but are otherwise similar to* Brochis. *Photo: Andre Roth.*

Corydoras bondi *belongs to the* aeneus-group *even though it resembles* trilineatus. *Photo: K. Paysan.*

up til 1980) includes: the **punctatus-group,** with *C. punctatus, C. armatus, C. ambiacus, C. trilineatus, C. amphibelus, C. agassizii, C. julii, C. multimaculatus, C. polystictus, C. melanistius melanistius, C. m. brevirostris, C. leopardus, C. reticulatus, C. leucomelas, C. sychri, C. concolor, C. caudimaculatus, C.* haraldschultzi, C. sterbai, C. schwartzi, C. evelynae, C. bicolor, C. surinamensis, C. atropersonatus, C. orphnopterus, C. acrensis, C. bifasciatus, C. ephippifer, C. xinguensis, C. pulcher, C. ornatus, and C. robustus; the **barbatus-group,** with *C. barbatus, C. paleatus, C. nattereri, C. erhardti, C. flaveolus, C. garbei, C. micracanthus, C.*

Corydoras trilineatus *is a member of the* punctatus-group. *It is distinguishable by the triple lateral stripe pattern. Photo: Andre Roth.*

One of the most spectacular species of Corydoras *is C. barbatus. The male (shown here) is much more colorful than the female. Photo: H.-J. Richter.*

macropterus, C. cochui, C. steindachneri, and *C. prionotos,* the **aeneus-group,** with *C. aeneus, C. eques, C. melanotaenia, C. metae, C. potaroensis, C. melini, C. arcuatus, C. bondi bondi, C. b. coppenamensis, C. griseus, C. rabauti, C. zygatus, C. osteocarus, C. reynoldsi, C. habrosus, C. axelrodi, C. boesemani, C. sanchesi, C. baderi, C. guianensis, C. heteromorphus, C. panda, C. weitzmani, C. gossei, C. oiapoquensis,* and *C. condiscipulus;* the **elegans-group,** with *C. elegans, C. hastatus, C. undulatus, C. latus, C. guapore, C. pygmaeus, C. nanus,* and *C. gracilis;* and the **acutus-group,** with *C. acutus, C.*

Corydoras paleatus *also belongs to the* barbatus-group *even though the two species look superficially different. Photo: Andre Roth.*

Corydoras semiaquilus *(*acutus-*group). Photo: Dr. Herbert R. Axelrod.*

Corydoras melanotaenia *(*aeneus-*group). Photo: Dr. Herbert R. Axelrod.*

Corydoras *sp. (*eques*?) (*aeneus-*group). Photo: K. Paysan.*

Corydoras prionotus *(barbatus-group)*. Photo: K. Paysan.

Corydoras polystictus *(punctatus-group)*. Photo: H.-J. Richter.

Corydoras polystictus *(punctatus-group)*. Photo: Harald Schultz.

Corydoras ambiacus (punctatus-*group*). Photo: K. Paysan.

Corydoras *sp.* Photo: Dr. Herbert R. Axelrod.

Corydoras trilineatus (punctatus-*group*). Photo: K. Paysan.

Corydoras melanistius melanistius *(punctatus-group)*. Photo: Dr. Herbert R. Axelrod.

Corydoras melanistius brevirostris *(punctatus-group)*. Photo: K. Paysan.

Corydoras sodalis *(punctatus-group)*. Photo: K. Paysan.

Corydoras simulatus *of the* acutus-group. *A dark band along the back from dorsal to caudal occurs in several different species of* Corydoras. *Photo: H.-J. Richter.*

aurofrenatus, C. treitlii, C. spilurus, C. septentrionalis, C. ellisae, C. fowleri, C. cervinus, C. pastazensis pastazensis, C. p. orcesi, C. semiaquilus, C. oxyrhynchus, C. octocirrus, C. saramaccensis, C. simulatus, C. maculifer, C. blochi blochi, C. b. vittatus, C. amapaensis, C. ourastigma, and *C. narcissus.*

Members of the genus *Corydoras* are distributed over South America from southeastern Brazil, Uruguay, and northern Argentina to the Guianas, Venezuela, and Colombia, and Trinidad. They seem to prefer slowly moving almost still (but seldom stagnant) streams and small rivers where the water is shallow (only to 2 meters in Surinam according to Nijssen) and very clear. The preferred bottom seems to be sand, but this may vary with species and area and the bottom may be pure sand or sand mixed with mud, and it may be covered with detritus and dead leaves. The banks and sides of the streams are covered with a luxuriant growth of plants, and this is where the corys are found. The temperature range depends of course upon the individual species and their respective ranges and altitudes, with the minimums for the temperate and high altitude species about 10° to 12°C and the maximum for the more tropical species to 32°C. With such a widespread distribution both horizontally and vertically (they are found to heights of over 3,000 meters), the corys inhabit a wide variety of water types but generally seem to prefer soft, neutral to slightly acidic or slightly alkaline pH (in Surinam, Nijssen reports they are found in slightly acidic waters of pH 5.3-6.7, not in the very acid tea-colored creeks with a pH of 4.6 or lower), and a hardness of 5-10°DH. They have a limited tolerance to salt (though most species can tolerate normal amounts used in aquaria) and are absent from the lowland coastal areas that are subject to tidal influences. Many species are commonly seen in schools or aggregations of hundreds to even thousands of individuals including males, females, and juveniles. Although they prefer their own company and the schools are mostly of a single species, other species can sometimes be seen mixed in.

The corys usually will be milling about the bottom (a few species such as *C. hastatus* spend more of their time in mid-water) searching for food, stirring up the bottom as they do. Their main food is bottom-dwelling insects and insect larvae and various worms, but at least some vegetable matter is also necessary. Although no corys are piscivorous, they will eat flesh from dead fishes. Their feeding method is to search the bottom with their sensory barbels and pick up food items with their mouth, often burying their snout up to their eyes. Long-snouted forms are better suited for this manner of feeding and perhaps can reach a different food supply than the short-snouted forms that are relegated to the upper surface layers. *Corydoras* are not restricted to this type feeding and many, as well as some from other

An aquarium filtered by an undergravel filter. The filter is shown partially exposed for illustrative purposes; under regular aquarium conditions the entire filter plate would be covered by gravel.

This tank is planted solely with rooted plants and has no floating plants; extensive open area in the foreground allows obstruction-free swimming space.

families, will feed from the surface layers by inverting themselves like the upside-down catfishes of the family Mochokidae. Others will feed on animals that live on the surface of the plant leaves. Corys seem to find their food by means of chemical "odors," for although food may be dropped literally in front of their noses they may ignore it completely until they can follow the scent right to the food.

Most of the callichthyids are able to survive in less than ideal conditions (polluted waters, low oxygen waters, or even when the shallow waters that they live in dry up) by their ability to utilize atmospheric air. As corys dart about on the bottom searching for food, they will suddenly stop and dash upward to the water's surface and quickly return to the bottom. This may be done in a quick straight dash or the fish

may rise partway in the water, hover for a moment, and then finish the trip. Even the downward movements may be rapid or at a more leisurely pace. Air is taken into the mouth at the surface and released through the anus on the downward trip. The movement may be by an individual fish, by a group of fish that break the surface, or by the original fish only breaking the surface, its followers just along for the ride so to speak and never reaching the surface. If the oxygen dissolved in the water is very low, preventing the catfish from reaching the surface can cause its death by suffocation. If the oxygen level is sufficient, however, preventing the catfish from reaching the surface will do it no harm as its branchial breathing is quite sufficient for sustaining life. In fact, this could be a good barometer in assessing the pollution in your aquarium. If the corys start to depend more and more on aerial respiration, it is evidence that an immediate water change should be made and a search for the reason(s) for this pollution must be started. It has also been found that aerial respiration is probably more important to the shallow water corys; this makes sense when one thinks about the energy that must be expended in reaching the surface from the greater depths as well as the longer time the fish is exposed to possible predation in the more open mid- and upper water layers.

Although the corys do not seem to be able to traverse "dry" land as well as the callichthyins, they are quite able to make shorter overland journeys when their water hole dries up.

Corys generally spawn right after the dry season (April or May in Surinam according to Nijssen), for with the rise in water level many more suitable spawning sites become available and there is an abundance of food for the fry that is washed down into the creeks from the land.

Finally, the intensity of colors of many of the species varies depending upon the type and the color of the bottom they are presently over. This is in addition to the high degree of variability of the color pattern in some of the species. It is quite possible that because of these variations many of the so-called "species" may turn out to be merely variants of one or another of the older species. So far only two species, *C. aeneus* and *C. paleatus,* are known to have albino forms commonly available.

It is generally accepted that the first exportation of a *Corydoras*

FTFFA winner. Corydoras aeneus, *best in* Corydoras *and other Cat- fishes category. Photo: Harry Grier.*

species was as early as 1880, when *C. paleatus* was shipped from the La Plata region to Europe; it arrived in North America at a later date, around 1915. Most of the *Corydoras* species are hardy and highly adaptable to most aquarium conditions and are almost always sought out to be members of a community tank because of their reputation for helping to keep the tank clean. Whether one calls

problem is usually to get enough food past the faster and heavier feeders of the upper layers. If corys are left to feed on only the "leftovers" of other fishes (providing there are any) they may find this diet inadequate and become listless and hollow-bellied. It is best to have a particular section of the tank where the corys can be hand-fed. The diet should be as varied as possible, preferably a good

Corydoras paleatus is sold as the Peppered Cory. It is easy to keep, easy to breed, and attractive as well. Photo: H.-J. Richter.

them scavengers or bottom cleaners, the fact remains that they do eat food items that reach the bottom and are quite adept at finding small food items that fall between the gravel particles and that are otherwise lost in nooks and crannies of the decorations. They do not eat droppings of other fishes. These must be siphoned out or if the volume is extremely small can be left in the tank to provide fertilizer for the plants. What is not used by the plants must be then broken down by the biological filter. The

meaty food base with some vegetable matter. Live foods are very much preferred, with tubificid worms heading the list, but frozen and freeze-dried foods and even a good flake food are suitable. Remember, when they are very hungry they do not hesitate to come up to the surface and feed inverted on anything floating there.

Any size aquarium can be used for housing these droll little catfishes, but a minimum size of five gallons for a single pair of one of the smaller species is

There are several species of dwarf Corydoras. *Among the most available is* C. hastatus. *Photo: A. van den Nieuwenhuizen.*

recommended. In very cramped quarters they tend to become somewhat sluggish. For the pygmy species *(C. pygmaeus, C. hastatus,* etc.) a 2-1/2 gallon tank is sufficient. A shallow tank is preferred to a deeper tank since they will come to the surface occasionally for a gulp of air. The bottom material should not be extremely coarse and sharp edges should be avoided (quartz and marble clips usually have sharp edges and should not be used). The substrate should not be too fine (silica sand is bad because it packs too tightly) or too coarse. A coarse grade of builder's sand (#6) or #4 red flint river gravel has been suggested as good substrates. Good filtration is highly recommended, the choice being up to the individual tastes. Driftwood pieces are often used with good results, and the tank should be heavily planted, leaving an open area for feeding and for

Corydoras adolfoi was spawned soon after sufficient numbers were made available to aquarists. It is popular but importations are sporadic. Photo: Dr. Herbert R. Axelrod.

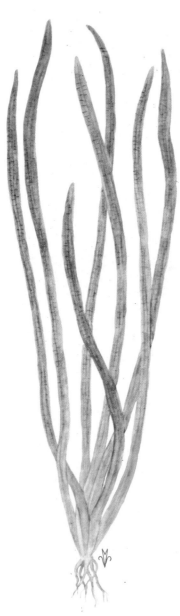

Rooted plants as this Sagittaria isoetiformis *are acceptable in a cory tank.*

swimming. Smooth-edged rocks can also be used. Among the suggested plants for corys are those that are native to their natural habitat. Those suggested include bunch plants such as *Elodea, Cabomba, Myriophyllum, Bacopa,* and *Ceratophyllum,* and rooted plants such as the swordplants, *Vallisneria, Sagittaria,* etc. Everything should be placed so that the effect is pleasing to the eye while it also provides hiding places for the shy species. When frightened, some corys will hide in small spaces and spread their sharp pectoral and dorsal spines.

The water itself can vary widely in its chemistry, but a pH of 6-8 is best as is a temperature of 21° to 26°C and a hardness of about 100 ppm. Weekly partial water changes are strongly recommended. It has been reported that corys will go into shock when placed into unaged tap water with no regard to temperature differences. They will go into a faint and actually keel over, but with luck they will start to wiggle a bit after a while and eventually recover completely. Otherwise they are quite hardy and very disease resistant, possibly in part due to their armor plating.

Certain types of fungus do attack them when they are housed under adverse conditions such as poor diet, excessive detritus, stress, water too acid, etc. Fungus may also appear as a secondary infection if a cory has been attacked by a larger, aggressive species and damage has been done. Another problem is characterized by pressure of petechiae under the belly plates and is called "blood spots" by aquarists. There is no known cure. Although the corys may not manifest any sign of a particular disease that is occurring in one of their tanks, do not move them to a healthy tank, for they are known to be carriers.

Caution should be exercised when handling corys. Like many

other catfishes with strong spines, they can damage each other when too crowded in a shipment or puncture the plastic bag so that all the water leaks out. They also cause problems when they are netted. If the spines get stuck in your net your first attempt to free them should be to invert the net in the aquarium and let them try to extricate themselves; this frequently works. If you must free them by hand be very careful, even cutting the net away if you have to.

These little catfishes are commonly very shy and will frequently hide among your plants and other decorations. It is highly recommended that they be kept in groups of at least a half

Two at first glance nearly identical species, Corydoras sterbai *(above)* and C. haraldschultzi *(below). Looking at the head, however, one sees a reverse pattern — white spots on dark and dark spots on light — for the two fishes. Photos: H.-J. Richter (above); Harald Schultz (below).*

61

Another striped cory. But notice in this C. schwartzi *none of the dark lines extend along the body where the two sets of plates meet. Photo: H.-J. Richter.*

dozen individuals. Even when the species are mixed they will aggregate when foraging or resting. In general, some corys will spend most of the day foraging for food while others will remain in seclusion, usually in an area of subdued light such as under the broad leaf of a plant. Corys should not be placed in a community tank that contains large, aggressive fishes·such as cichlids and large barbs, but with smaller non-aggressive species such as small characins, livebearers, and possibly rasboras.

In addition to all their good points corys have also been said to destroy unwanted planaria and to clean up the blue-green algae infesting a tank, neither of which I have been able to confirm. But they are one of the most popular of the catfishes for not only are they peaceful, harmless, of an excellent size for aquaria, hardy, and spawnable, but they also "wink" at their owners from time to time. Actually it is not a true wink, but the rapid movement when the eyes are rotated (the eyes can be moved

independently) in their socket. Their hardiness borders on legend, for there are reports of one species known to survive temperatures up to 40°C and another (possibly *C. paleatus)* whose eggs hatched out at a very chilly 7°C. Longevity records are also amazing, for *C. aeneus* is said to have lived 27 years in captivity and 20 years is not too uncommon.

Most corys are currently still being shipped in from South America even though there are export restrictions on some species by several countries. Be wary of some of the imports, for improper conditions at the holding stations in some areas (usually overcrowding with some fouling of the water) cause stress and this may lead to hemorrhaging; if there are any disease organisms or parasites infecting the fishes they may become more dangerous to the weakened fishes. One more item—since corys are able to utilize atmospheric air they should not be shipped in bags loaded with pure oxygen (this is also true of the labyrinthfishes such as

Corydoras evelynae *was named for Mrs. Evelyn Axelrod. It is distin-guishable by the broken band along the back from dorsal to caudal fin. Photo: Dr. Herbert R. Axelrod.*

gouramis) lest it cause damage to the fish's delicate air breathing apparatus.

Of all the *Corydoras* species *C. aeneus* and *C. paleatus* are the most common. Indeed, the latter species has the distinction of having been discovered by none other than Charles Darwin on his famous voyage of the *Beagle* over 150 years ago. Both of these species are bred commercially by the hundreds of thousands, *C. aeneus* mostly in the United States, *C. paleatus* in Europe. Albinos of both species have been successfully bred and in some cases are more popular than the original pigmented fishes. In addition to the two just mentioned, hobbyists have bred a large percentage of the species of *Corydoras* (at least 40%) in home aquaria. A partial list of

This well marked species, Corydoras axelrodi, *was named for Dr. Her-bert R. Axelrod, himself. Photo: H.-J. Richter.*

Corydoras nattereri is more attractive than the photo indicates. In the right light the lateral stripe shimmers with almost a neon green color. Photo: H.-J. Richter.

these species includes *aeneus, paleatus, hastatus, "schultzei" (aeneus), arcuatus, undulatus, melanistius, metae, elegans, cochui, panda, adolfoi, reticulatus, rabauti, barbatus, axelrodi, pygmaeus, schwartzi, bondi, habrosus, melanotaenia, nattereri, ornatus, amapaensis, eques, macropterus, agassizii, leucomelas, caudimaculatus, haraldschultzi, trilineatus, boesemani,* and *sterbai.* They were spawned under a variety of conditions, and accounts will be discussed under the individual species when known. In general, however, there are some similarities or generalities that can be reported here. Although

One of the many variations in the color pattern of Corydoras reticulatus. *It almost appears as if this were a mixture of several other species of cory. Photo: Andre Roth.*

some corys are thought to be relatively easy to spawn and others relatively hard, depending of course upon the aquarist's skill and luck, it is not as easy to spawn corys as some of the beginner's fishes that will spawn almost anywhere anytime, like white clouds or zebra danios. It does take some care and preparation and a lot of patience to spawn corys, but once they have started they seem to do so on a regular basis. One aquarist even reports that once started they are hard to turn off. The viewed from above it can be seen that the females are distinctly heavier across the body at the level of the pectoral fins; if viewed from the side they appear to have a deeper body and may bulge in the ventral surface area if they are ripe with eggs (in some cases, especially albinos, the eggs may be visible through the skin). The males may also have longer and more pointed ventral fins and slightly longer dorsal and pectoral fin spines or higher dorsal fins. In a few species the males are larger, in others they

One of the Corydoras aeneus *lookalikes,* C. melanotaenia. *The relatively bar-like greenish band is the tip-off for identification. Photo: H.-J. Richter.*

general concensus is that one must use two males for every female in the spawning tank. Some say three males per female should be used and others just state that the more males per female the better, so the 2:1 ratio might be regarded as a minimum with additional males added when possible.

Sexing corys is not too difficult with mature fish. If a number of them are placed together and have bristles on their cheeks, and in still others there may be a color difference between the two sexes. If you are not sure you can always use the tried and true method of starting with at least a half dozen individuals and letting them sort things out for themselves. Of course the male to female ratio may not be ideal using this method.

The tank size does not seem to be very important as success has been achieved with a trio (two males and one female) in a five gallon tank. Larger species of course would necessarily require larger tanks. The tank should be shallow and have a dark bottom — either bare slate or a layer of dark-colored sand or gravel. Provide hiding places, usually in the form of plants, such

This last is most likely involved with observations that some spawnings have occurred during periods of major changes in atmospheric pressure. The temperature changes, when and if made, should be gradual enough so that the fish are not stressed. One aquarist advocates simply unplugging the heater and

Corydoras erhardti has a distinctive pattern. Nevertheless, if this species is mixed in with other similar species it could easily be overlooked. Photo: S. Itsukusima.

as broad-leaved Amazon sword plants and/or some bunch plants. Filtration and aeration are necessary. In fact, some aquarists believe that added aeration will help bring the fish into a spawning mood more quickly. Weekly water changes are also advised. Beyond these suggestions for inducement of spawning there have been several "sure-fire" methods that are advocated by one aquarist or another. These include things like sudden drops or sudden changes both up and down (a fluctuation) of the water temperature and sprinkling the surface with water using a watering can to simulate the onset of the rainy season.

letting the water cool to room temperature naturally over several days' time. The temperature differences should be no more than 3° to 8°C. None of the above methods are surefire. Under reasonable conditions with healthy breeders they will go ahead and spawn, especially if they are domestically bred, even in a community tank, although chances are that under such conditions the spawning is rarely observed and the eggs are quickly disposed of by the other fishes. One thing that must be done is to properly condition the potential spawners. This means a high protein diet of live foods, preferably tubificid worms.

Two Corydoras *species that might be confused,* C. pastazensis *(above) and* C. septentrionalis *(below). This latter species has recently become more available in the northeastern U. S. Photos: K. Paysan (above); H.-J. Richter (below).*

Chopped earthworms and a good flake food can be added for variety. Feed small amounts several times a day. The length of the conditioning period varies depending upon the species being spawned, their health at the time of the start of conditioning, and the type of food fed, and may last for as little as two to three days to as much as a month or more. All this providing, of course, that the corys are fully mature and able to spawn.

The first indication that something is about to happen is an increased activity, for the actual spawning is usually preceded by a rather long courtship period. These normally slow, albeit nervous, fishes suddenly become quite frisky, dashing about back and forth and up and down. The females are usually in front and the males

67

Corydoras acutus *is not commonly available to aquarists. Its care and breeding are much the same as the other corys. Photo: Dr. S. Weitzman.*

behind. Although this has often been described as a chase by the males, one aquarist has noted that in his courting corys the males were hard put to keep up with the females. This procession proceeds all over the tank as the males do some little dances in front of the females. The females, as they become more and more interested in the actions of the males and hence in spawning, will pay attention to prospective spawning sites. These may be on leaves, rocks, driftwood, filters, heaters, glass tank sides, or anything solid that attracts them. Cleaning now starts. This may be accomplished solely by the females or in some instances the males take part and help clean. Most species prefer a site off the bottom but well below the surface of the water; however, other species prefer higher or lower localities. Specific preferences will be noted under the species accounts when known. Regardless of the substrate or level selected, an area near an airstone is commonly preferred. In addition to the interruptions for cleaning of the spawning sites,

both males and females will make short dashes to the surface for air with a frequency somewhat greater than their normal habit. Sites that were cleaned may be revisited for some "touching up."

After all of this lively dashing about things become more serious. The males seem to pay particular attention to an area behind the female's head as they swim over her back. As they swim in this position there is an occasional contact with the barbels on the suprascapular region of the female. This was described by one aquarist as a "kiss" of sorts. The males also nudge or butt the females on the sides and head as the female swims among them with her barbels feeling about. Actual spawning then commences.

The early morning hours are the most popular spawning time for many species, but some have been seen to spawn even during late evening hours. When the female is "satisfied" that everying is in readiness she may turn around and start chasing the males. It is at this time that the famous "T" position is assumed.

In all the chasing and moving about the excited female will sometimes, but not always, position herself so that she will be nudging or pushing at the side of the male near his vent with her head, her barbels very active. Although it is usually the female that initiates this action, in some cases it is the male who will place himself in front of the female, soliciting her attention.

Occasionally the males of some species will, in their excited state, use their mouth to attach themselves to almost any part of the female. In the "T" position, however, the male may become "paralyzed with ecstacy" and roll over slightly as the female nudges him and he clasps her barbels to his side with his strong pectoral spines. Locked in this position the partners quiver a bit as the eggs and sperm are released. The "T" position then acts as a stimulus for the simultaneous release of the sexual products. The close proximity of the pair, along with the movements of the fish, their gill movements, their fin movements, and the amount of sperm released (a cloud surrounding the two fishes is usual), serves to ensure that the eggs are properly fertilized. Other theories involving sperm passing into the mouth of the female and out the gills to the eggs, sperm taken into the female's mouth for later fertilization of the eggs as they are deposited on the cleaned sites, and sperm smeared on the female's barbels for later fertilization at the site of egg-laying all seem to be less plausible. In fact, in some instances the "T" position is not assumed and egg laying and fertilization are accomplished just as well while the pair are parallel to each other or belly to belly as they both roll on their sides.

A pair of Corydoras aeneus *in the "T" position. Although this usually takes place on the bottom, this one is occurring in midwater. Photo by R. Zukal.*

A female Corydoras aeneus *carrying eggs in her ventral fin "basket". As can be seen, only a few eggs are laid at a time. Photo: R. Zukal.*

The "T" position (or other spawning position) lasts approximately 10 to 20 seconds, during which time it is difficult to disturb them. The female ejects anywhere from one to many eggs into a special pouch formed by the juxtaposition of her ventral fins, and with the cloud of sperm surrounding the pair they are immediately fertilized. As this is happening the other male or males are swimming about excitedly and may even approach the spawners and touch them with their barbels. Actually only a single male is involved in the fertilization of a batch of eggs, but the next spawning bout may involve one of the other males. With the eggs safely ensconced in the ventral fin pouch, the female frees herself from the male and may rest a moment or may immediately start off looking for a place where her eggs may

be deposited. She may carry the eggs about for several minutes until finally settling on the "proper" spot for her eggs. This is usually one of the previously cleaned sites, but she may also decide to clean a new one for that particular batch of eggs. The site chosen varies widely with species. Some prefer midwater sites, some like the area near the surface, some like stones, others glass, others leaves of plants, and still others seem to scatter them all over the tank. Actually "scatter" is not the proper word for these fishes nor is substrate spawner; perhaps they should best be called egg depositors. Some species might deposit all eggs of the entire spawn at one site; others place small batches at different sites throughout the aquarium, whether carefully selected or purely at random.

The small batches usually

number from a single egg to as many as 30 or so depending upon the particular species involved. The eggs are pushed onto the substrate that is finally selected by the female as she glides over the spot, belly to the surface. The adhesive eggs stick tightly in place. It is interesting to speculate as to why the eggs stick so well to the smooth glass walls of the aquarium but not to the fins that envelop them. Perhaps the mucous coating of the female's fins prevents this or perhaps a special fluid is secreted to prevent their sticking to the fins. The eggs vary in size from 1.2 to 2.0 mm and are generally opaque (whitish or light colored but becoming dark as development proceeds).

As the female is placing the eggs, the males are usually following her about ready for the next spawning bout. Spawning times and activity vary depending on the species, perhaps lasting a few hours, perhaps lasting intermittently over a whole week. The bouts ("T" position) are repeated over and over again (one aquarist estimated 30-50 times) until the female is depleted of eggs. If several males are involved they probably all will have taken their turns to fertilize the female's eggs. Some spawners are deceptive in that they may spawn a few eggs on one day and then rest, seemingly finished with spawning. The next day the bulk of the eggs may be laid or another short spawning bout may occur, the big spawning held off until the third day. Many unknowing aquarists, observing the spawning on the first day, may assume spawning has been completed and most of the eggs

Eggs are deposited on all sorts of objects in the aquarium including, as seen here, the glass sides of the tank. The eggs adhere tightly to the smooth glass. Photo: H.-J. Richter.

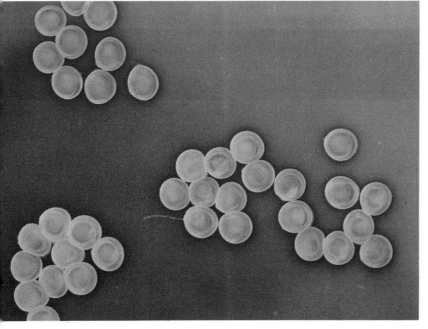

eaten and remove the spawners before the real spawning has gotten underway. Check the female to see if she looks depleted. If she is still rotund and appears full of eggs, have patience. When the corys are at their spawning peak they will be spawning every 2 to 3 minutes, with very few rest periods in between. When several hundred eggs have been deposited, the females appear empty of eggs, and both sexes seem to lose interest in each other and begin their food searching, rooting about in the bottom material, spawning is most likely finished.

Depending upon species and the level of hunger in the spawners, the parents may eat the eggs or may not. Although many well fed corys will not eat their eggs, some will, or they may ignore the eggs but finish off the fry. Since this behavior varies not only with the species involved but also with individuals, it might be best to separate spawners from the spawn. The eggs are fairly tough and may be scraped from their place of attachment without damage or, easier still, the adult fishes may be removed and the eggs hatched in the tank where they were spawned. This may be preferable especially when the eggs are spawned on rocks or other places from which they are difficult to remove. The eggs can be placed in gallon jars or relatively small aquaria to hatch. The addition of some acriflavine or methylene blue helps control fungus and an airstone is suggested. The number of eggs deposited varies with the species and the size and health of the spawners. Some species lay only about 30 eggs, others as many as 800, with 200 to 300 being average. It has been suggested that the eggs be kept protected from bright lights. Depending upon species and the temperature, the eggs will hatch

Corydoras *fry already searching for food along the bottom. Their tiny but well developed barbels can even be seen. These are albino* C. aeneus *fry. Photo: G. Padovani.*

Corydoras leucomelas *(above) and* C. *sp.(possibly* orphnopterus*)(below).* C. leucomelas *has a dark dorsal blotch that extends onto the back. Photos: K. Paysan.*

in anywhere from two or three to eight to ten days. Just prior to hatching the fry can be seen moving about within the egg. There is no parental care of eggs or fry.

At the time of hatching the fry, by vigorous wriggling, break through the egg membrane and fall to the bottom. The newly hatched fry appear as tiny slivers with all the fins connected like those of a tadpole. If gravel is present in their hatching tank they will be very hard to see for a couple of days. The yolk sac is absorbed in about two or three days, at which time food should be offered. Actually, during the first couple of days after hatching a few drops of liquid fry food can be added to promote a growth of infusoria. After this, microworms, newly hatched brine shrimp, and

73

powdered flake food that has been wetted down to make it sink are fed on a regular schedule. Growth is fairly rapid under proper conditions and they soon will have to be moved to larger quarters. Growth is also augmented if there is a fine coating of filamentous green algae on the glass sides of the tank that the fry can feed from. These active fry do consume a lot of food for their size and sufficient food must be available for them at all times, yet not so much food that the tank becomes foul. Too small a raising tank becomes foul quickly, too large a tank means that the fry have to search further afield for the food and may even starve in the process. A 10-gallon tank has been suggested as ideal for this purpose. A sponge filter will help keep pollution under

Corydoras ornatus *(above) and* C. loxozonus *(below). With more than 100 species of* Corydoras *already described, the total number eventually may reach as high as 150. Photos: Dr. Herbert R. Axelrod (above); Aaron Norman (below).*

Corydoras osteocarus *can also be called a peppered cory because of its spotted pattern. This species is not usually available to aquarists. Photo: Andre Roth.*

control as will the addition of a few freshwater snails such as *Pomacea* once the fry are mobile enough. Once the yolk has been absorbed the fry will be seen skipping or hopping over the bottom, but they soon become more proficient swimmers.

Remember, catfish babies feed from the bottom and brine shrimp may wind up throughout the water column. This can be rectified by placing a small light (not too bright) near the bottom to attract the baby brine to the vicinity of the hungry catfish fry. It has been reported that catfish fry die from too much salt being added with the brine shrimp if they are not thoroughly rinsed before being fed. This has been disputed, the deaths being attributed to velvet possibly introduced with the brine shrimp or due to uneaten food decaying in the tank.

Since the fry are very susceptible to fouled water (as are adults) periodic water changes are highly recommended. Some suggest daily water changes, some

weekly, but in either case the water should be aged at least 24 hours under aeration before use. In a short time the fry are ready for chopped tubificid worms. Other recommendations include a low light level and some hiding places. The water in the raising tank should be relatively shallow at first. One can actually start with a 15 or 20 gallon tank with a small portion of it filled with water. As the fry get larger the water level can be raised accordingly, thus making it unnecessary to move them to larger quarters — they are already there! The critical period is the first three weeks. The water level can be raised about 2 cm every time the water is changed, ideally every third day or so. As the fry grow it is natural that some will do better than others. The aquarist must keep a wary eye on them and start sorting them early. With growth the catfish's menu can grow also, both in size and variety. Although most adult corys will accept baby brine, microworms, etc., they can also receive live tubificid worms, adult

An unusual pattern for Corydoras aeneus *with the dark lateral blotch restricted to the anterior portion of the body. Photo: B. Kahl.*

brine shrimp, whiteworms, and even flake food.

Meanwhile, the parents are probably ready to spawn again and the whole process can be repeated. Most adults spawn regularly over a period of several months and then should be rested. The spawning bouts are a week to ten days apart and there may be several spawning periods within a year.

Corydoras aeneus and *C. paleatus* are by far the most common species in the hobby today. They are both easily bred and are produced in commercial quantities in the United States, Europe, and Singapore. Most of the available fish are therefore domestic strains. Any wild imports are reported to be less easy to breed.

Corydoras aeneus was first discovered in clear streams in Trinidad, the original home of the guppy, but appears to be a fairly widespread and complex species covering much of tropical South America. This species is easy to keep and is commonly kept in community tanks as a scavenger. It requires no specific conditions, but very acid water should be avoided. It does best in a temperature range of 18° to 26°C and on a diet of mostly live foods, particularly tubificid worms, enchytrae, and chironomid larvae. *C. aeneus* also does best when kept in small groups of its own kind.

Spawning follows the above routine fairly closely (much of the general discussion was based on *aeneus* and *paleatus* behavior) with the actual spawning precipitated by a drop in water temperature, a large water change, or the fish starting to spawn spontaneously. For those who advocated a temperature drop, usually about 5°C, the best method was to unplug the heater and let the water cool slowly and naturally. Some made a water change but the new water was purposefully about 5° cooler than the aquarium water. Others moved the spawners to a new tank. Although those advocating the more drastic methods say no harm came to their fish, it is still a risky proposition. With healthy, mature, well-conditioned adults a normal water change should be enough of a stimulus.

C. aeneus seems to prefer spawning on a flat surface, commonly utilizing the glass sides of the aquarium or the plastic filter box if an inside filter is used (a sponge filter would be better). As many as 500 to 600 eggs have been reported spawned in a group spawning situation, but the average is closer to 200 to 300 eggs for a normal spawn. Anywhere from 5-15 eggs are dropped each time a "T" position is assumed. Many aquarists leave the parents in with the eggs and fry as this species is less inclined than other species to eat either. However, it has been known to happen and the aquarist must decide for himself. The hatching period depends upon the temperature and may take anywhere from

Increased activity may indicate the approach of spawning. Males swim about females nudging them or caressing them with body and fins. These Corydoras aeneus *seem about to spawn. Photo: H.-J. Richter.*

Once things get serious the "T" position is assumed and actual egglaying and their fertilization occurs. In the upper photo the male's pectoral fin is clasping the barbels of the female. The lower photo shows the beginning of another "T" after some eggs (on glass and plants) have been deposited. Photos: H.-J. Richter.

The female catches the eggs in her clasped ventral fins and swims about the tank to previously cleaned spots where they are deposited. Here more eggs are being stuck to the glass side of the tank. Photo: H.-J. Richter.

79

Corydoras aeneus *in "T" position. Photo: A. Roth.*

C. aeneus *variety. Photo: Ken Lucas, Steinhart Aquarium.*

C. latus. *Photo: Dr. Herbert R. Axelrod.*

Closeup of head of C. aeneus. *Photo: Andre Roth.*

Albino C. aeneus. *Photo: Andre Roth.*

C. aeneus *var. Photo: K. Paysan.*

81

Group spawnings are the norm for Corydoras *breeding. Here a group of albino* C. aeneus *have started their activity. Photo: G. Padovani.*

three to four days to a week; the hatching at three days was at a temperature of 28°C, the longer periods at about 20°C. The fry when first hatched will drop to the bottom of the tank and burrow into the gravel so that they are very difficult to see. In a few days they are moving about searching for food and can be fed microworms and newly hatched brine shrimp. The fry are said to be somewhat sensitive to temperature and water changes.

The albino *C. aeneus,* as expected, differ very little if at all in their behavior from the normally colored individuals. Some say the fry are a little slower to develop than the regular *aeneus,* others say the albinos are practically blind and the males sometimes sterile. This might be caused by inbreeding too extensively and does not apply to all the albinos in the hobby but perhaps only to a small portion of them. As the female albinos fill with eggs the belly starts to take on a pinkish or rosy hue due to the blood vessels that

are more visible with the expanded body walls.

Many aquarists advise getting young *aeneus* (about six months old or so) and raising them to maturity (about 2-2 1/2 years old) for best spawning results.

Corydoras aeneus seems to have a number of lookalikes that use its name in the hobby whether deliberately or by simple misidentification. *Brochis* species are often called giant *aeneus;* and the green-gold *aeneus* from Colombia has turned out to be a different species, *C. melanotaenia.* It is hoped that at some early date this complex species will be studied in earnest and its mysteries revealed.

Corydoras paleatus originates from the slow-moving waters of southern Brazil and northern Argentina. The female is slightly larger then the male, attaining a length of about 7 cm to the male's 5 cm. The fish in the hobby are virtually all commercially bred and wild-caught individuals are no longer seen, though it is reported that they are more colorful than the aquarium strains, most of which now come from Singapore. There is an albino *C. paleatus,* but this is not seen very often. It is easily distinguishable from the *aeneus* albino because the pattern of *paleatus* is still present while the *aeneus* albino is very plain.

Spawning has been accomplished in captivity for this species for over a century. The behavior follows the above procedures fairly closely as this species was, along with *C. aeneus,* used as a model. There are no specific conditions needed by *C. paleatus* for keeping or breeding, and it does well in a community tank. Some aquarists suggest a 50% water change a week, others more, and still others less. The proper temperature range is 18° to 20°C

but it will live at lower temperatures (to 15°C) and at higher temperatures (to 23°C), but at the higher temperatures there are many more trips to the surface for air and usually it will not breed. The spawning tank should have some natural gravel (no black gravel please) and be planted (perhaps with *Aponogeton* and/or *Hygrophila)* or bare. Some indirect sunlight is permissible. The potential spawners should be conditioned for at least two weeks on a high-protein diet. As the female fills with eggs her belly can be seen changing to a pinkish or salmon color. It has been suggested that the sexes should be conditioned separately for best results. Since the temperature drops during the rainy season (which is the spawning season for these fish),

A male C. paleatus *courting a female by swimming above her and caressing the top of her head with his barbels. Photo: H.-J. Richter.*

As the excitement builds other individuals become involved. Here two males are courting the same female. Photo: H.-J. Richter.

a stimulus for spawning is a drop in water temperature (as noted above) or a large water change, or both. A six to eight degree change is sufficient. Two or more males (these are smaller and with higher and more pointed dorsal fins) are used for each female.

Spawning usually takes place over several days, with the largest batch deposited on the second or third day. The initial batches of eggs will probably be eaten. Since most of the spawning activity occurs in the morning hours an evening feeding has been suggested. A feeding during the spawning might disrupt the spawners. The "T" position is generally assumed, but the female will also attach herself to the male's side

or belly with her mouth at times. About four to six eggs are released into the fin pouch, although some estimates run as high as 20 or as low as one egg. In one report the female was said to move backward over the bottom to scoop up the eggs that were dropped. The eggs are deposited in the higher levels of the tank, usually at some distance from the bottom. If plants are present eggs may also be deposited on the leaves (it should be noted that the corys will not place eggs on unhealthy plants), again in the upper levels. The number of eggs spawned seems to average about 250 to 300 (one aquarist reported 372 eggs deposited in 3 1/2 hours!). Infertile eggs turn a bluish white

The "T" position is eventually assumed and the male clasps the female's barbels with his ventral fin. Photo: H.-J. Richter.

in methleyne blue treated water after a few hours while the healthy eggs remain a creamy white. Hatching time varied from a low of two days to a high of 14 days, but the majority of reports claim four to seven days as average, depending upon temperature.

Feeding the fry is as above. The newly hatched fry are a light (about 15% or so) are recommended, and gentle aeration is beneficial to keep the surface as clean as possible for the time (about six to eight weeks) when the young catfishes first start to take air from the surface. For this reason the water depth should not be too great, at least for the first couple of months. The parents may be

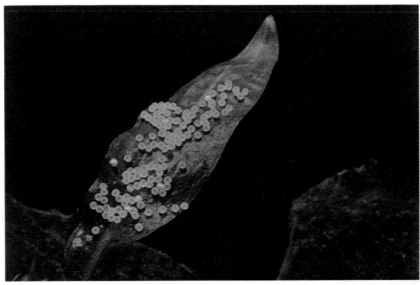

Eggs are deposited on various objects depending upon species. Some select only broad plant leaves as seen here. Photo: R. Zukal.

brown in color and with the continuous fins look like tiny tadpoles. They are light-sensitive and burrow into the gravel or seek out the darkest spots in the aquarium. After about a week, however, with the yolk all used up and the search for food beginning, they take on a dark, almost black, color. In about five weeks they start to become lighter in color again except for some darker patches over the body. At this time they should be at least 12 mm in length. Daily water changes in the fry tank allowed to spawn again in about three weeks. Because of the high temperatures, summertime spawning attempts are not likely to be successful.

Corydoras hastatus is a small (to about 35 mm) species from the Amazon basin to adjacent areas of Boliva and Paraguay. It differs from most *Corydoras* species by preferring the midwater areas, spending most of its time well off the bottom among the plants. When it does rest it does so on the available plant leaves still high above the bottom and is not adverse to inverting itself belly-up against the bottom of a leaf. All plants are utilized whether they are fine-leaved, as hornwort, or with broader leaves, as Amazon sword plants or *Sagittaria,* although the latter seem to be preferred, as is a position where they can remain horizontal to the bottom. They maintain themselves while swimming in the open water by rapid fin movements, principally of the pectoral fins. Its movements, combined with a high breathing rate, give the impression of a very nervous fish ceaselessly active, reminiscent of the well known hummingbirds. *C. hastatus* should only be kept in small groups, which immediately form into schools. In one instance there were only three *hastatus* in a tank. When two tetras that had patterns similar to those of the *hastatus* were added, the five

were soon swimming around the tank together, although the *Corydoras* would dash to the surface for a gulp of air from time to time. *C. hastatus* will feed both in midwater or on a substrate whether it is one of the plant leaves or actually on the bottom like other *Corydoras* species. There is no particular food preference other than live foods, but most frozen, freeze-dried, and flake foods are accepted. The aquarium need not be very large, a 5-gallon tank being quite sufficient for a small school of *C. hastatus.* The tank should be clean and well aerated and the water slightly alkaline (pH about 7.6) within a temperature range of 25° to 29°C. These peaceful, inoffensive little fish (aquarium specimens rarely exceed 25 mm total length) are good community tank fish and good scavengers for fry tanks.

Spawning has been

Corydoras hastatus is a dwarf species that spends much of its time in midwater. Small schools such as this one are recommended.

The pattern on the caudal base makes Corydoras hastatus *readily recognizable. Photo: H.-J. Richter.*

accomplished with this species, and the behavior follows that already outlined fairly closely. The spawning tank can be as small as 2 1/2 gallons but at least a 5-gallon tank is recommended. A small sponge filter and some plants should be added. No special water is needed other than it being aged. Since *hastatus* may spawn as a school the whole group can be conditioned for spawning. Be sure there are at least two males for every female. The males are more slender and have a more pointed dorsal fin. Condition with the usual tubificid and whiteworms and you will soon see the females getting quite plump. Cleaning of sites included the plant leaves, and after the usual courtship the "T" position was seen along with trembling of both sexes on the bottom of the tank. In contrast to the other species, however, only a single egg is extruded and fertilized. The female, carrying the egg in the ventral pouch, swam toward

the surface and deposited the adhesive egg on one of the plant leaves that was previously cleaned. The act was repeated about every three minutes for from one to two hours with 10- to 15-minute rests between the egg releases. Never was there more than a single egg released. About seven to ten eggs are spawned in a day (usually between 7 a.m. and 2 p.m.), and spawning occurs on three to four consecutive days. Very little food was accepted over the spawning period, but after they were finished they started looking for something to eat. A total of anywhere from 30 to 60 or more eggs may be spawned by a single female, but when a group spawns the total number may reach 300 or more depending upon how many females are present. If not enough suitable plants are available, the aquarium glass may be used as an egg deposition site (one aquarist reported eggs were placed anywhere and everywhere).

Eggs hatch in three to nine days (most report a hatch time of three to four days). The eggs start as tiny translucent spheres with a tiny dark spot in the center. As they develop they turn a light amber in color. The fry are about 6 mm long at hatching, mostly translucent but also with a dark spot or spotting. They were ready to accept newly hatched brine shrimp as well as microworms soon after they hatched. For a couple of weeks the fry are a dark olive with black blotches all over the body, but they then start to look more and more like their parents. In two months they are

Corydoras xinguensis *(above) received its specific name from the area of its capture, the Rio Xingu.* Corydoras atropersonatus *is rather non-descript and usually is found mixed with other corys that are imported. Photos: H.-J. Richter (above); Ed Taylor (below).*

about 18 mm long. They mature in six to eight months. The parents will be ready to spawn again in a couple of weeks. The parents remain very translucent, much like the glass cats of the genus *Kryptopterus* but with a large black marking on the caudal base. Myers (1953) erected the forth in the aquarium, they will occasionally come to rest on a leaf and have been likened to hummingbirds flitting from flower to flower. Single individuals do not do very well. A small group of at least half a dozen specimens is recommended, and because of its small size a dozen fish in a

Another pygmy Corydoras *that does better when kept in groups is* C. pygmaeus.

subgeneric name *Microcorydoras* for this species.

Corydoras pygmaeus is another dwarf species and attains a length of only about 3 cm. It is fairly widespread in South America but was originally discovered in the Rio Madeira system. Like *C. hastatus*, *C. pygmaeus* is more of a midwater species than a bottom-dwelling one. They swim out in the open by the rapid movements of their pectoral and caudal fins with the barbels held against the body. In this manner they can also remain in one spot, hovering so to speak, for as much as 30 seconds at a time. In their swimming back and tank is not unheard of. The tank should be at least 5 gallon capacity and provided with a sand or gravel substrate and be well planted. A few rocks (no sharp edges) and some driftwood can complete the decorations. If the tank is to be a community tank, perhaps some *Nannostomus* or small hatchetfishes, neons, or small *Rasbora* species can be added. A sponge filter and regular water changes help to keep the tank quite clean and well aerated. The water should then be glass-clear, have a German hardness of 2 to 8°, and a temperature of 24° to 26°C.

Corydoras pygmaeus *appears to be one of those species that will deposit their eggs only on plant leaves. Photo: H.-J. Richter.*

Some elements of their feeding behavior are quite different from the normal *Corydoras* feeding behavior. As they swim through the water they make sudden stops on one or another of the plant leaves and move about on the leaf as if "sniffing" at it. Actually they are searching for various microorganisms that they would normally find on the leaves in their normal habitat. Not only do they search the upper side of the leaves, but they will move to the underside of the leaf and give it a good going over as well. Since there will not be enough natural food in the aquarium, they

Corydoras gracilis *seems to be a dwarf species. This is a photo of one of the original specimens. Photo: H. Bleher.*

will need supplementary feedings of daphnia (they can catch these animals in midwater), baby brine shrimp, grindal worms, chironomid larvae, and tubificid worms, as well as some frozen, freeze-dried, and even flake foods. A lettuce leaf should be added from time to time. One report mentioned that when a ball of tubificid worms was fed and the *C. pygmaeus* first came into contact with it, the catfish darted around the tank as if frightened, but after several minutes they quieted down and started to feed. There was no explanation for this unusual behavior.

Of several spawning accounts recorded, the actual spawning behavior was not witnessed, but it was assumed to parallel quite closely that of *C. hastatus*. Water changes with cooler water are suggested in order to trigger the spawning, making sure of course that the temperature does not drop too low. The sexes should also be in a ratio of two males for each female. According to one account the best time of the year to spawn *C. pygmaeus* is from autumn to spring. Success for this aquarist was never achieved out of this time period. *C. pygmaeus* may have a specific spawning period or it may be that the summer temperatures are too high for it to spawn. Like *C. hastatus,* the eggs were deposited singly on plants throughout the aquarium; unlike *C. hastatus,* which would utilize the glass walls of the aquarium along with other objects, *C. pygmaeus* seems to accept only

Items meant to be sterilized by boiling water should be sterilized outside the tank, not in it, as boiling water could kill fish in the aquarium or shatter the tank itself.

Corydoras sychri *wears a dark mask across its eyes. This is apparently a protective adaptation. Photo: Dr. Herbert R. Axelrod.*

the plant leaves. *Hygrophila polysperma* appears to be preferred over other fine-leaved plants. Some 20 to 40 eggs were spawned, the eggs being about 2 mm and grayish with a brown luster. They are quite adhesive and can be removed and reattached in a more suitable place by the aquarist for about the first 24 hours. With time the adhesiveness decreases.

At 25°C the eggs hatch in 50 to 72 hours. They become darker and the egg membrane becomes clear enough so that the embryo can be seen prior to hatching. It sports a blackish zone immediately behind the small head. Upon hatching a large yolk sac is still evident and the pectoral fins are large and transparent. As the yolk is absorbed the black spot spreads out so that after 36 hours the yolk sac is much smaller and the black spot has spread out to form a band between the eyes. The body exhibits several (three?) vertical bars. After 72 hours feeding must start as the yolk sac

is depleted. With the water level quite low (to concentrate the food) microworms and baby brine shrimp can be introduced. Water changes and siphoning will help to keep the water clean. After a few weeks the young are colored much like the parents.

Corydoras metae is a small (to 6 cm) catfish from the Rio Meta system of Colombia. It is strikingly patterned and as such is usually in demand by aquarists. The body color may vary from a grayish to a tan depending upon their mood, and females commonly exhibit a golden pink tone over the entire body while the abdomen becomes rosy. The tank should be set up with the usual sand bottom, driftwood, rocks, etc., and should be well planted. For spawning, *Microsorium pteropus* (Java fern) and *Ceratopteris thalicroides* (water sprite) seem to be the favorites when they are allowed to float at the surface. The diet and conditioning foods are the same as recommended for *C. aeneus* and *C. paleatus*. The pH

The body of Corydoras metae *varies from grayish to tan depending upon mood, with females sometimes exhibiting a pinkish tone. Photo: H.-J. Richter.*

should be slightly on the acid side (one spawning was reported at 5.2), and the DH 4 or 5; the temperature range should be 23° to 26°C. Water changes of about 20 to 30% per week are recommended.

Spawning is similar to that of C. aeneus, with the chasing about the tank eventually ending in a "T" position. This is held for about five seconds and the pair then lie motionless for another 25 to 30 seconds or so. *Corydoras metae* will apparently release a single egg (about 2 mm) each time. If the tank is bare the glass walls of the tank are the

Corydoras metae *produces a single egg at a time which, if possible, is deposited on plant leaves. Photo: H. Linke.*

Corydoras melini *also has a dark stripe from dorsal to caudal, but in this species the angle differs and the caudal fin is involved. Photo: Dr. Herbert R. Axelrod.*

recipients of the eggs. However, if the "preferred" plants are available 90% of the eggs will be deposited on them. The underside of the plant leaves as well as the fine rootlets are utilized, and the eggs may be clustered in several spots, the eggs being placed there one at a time. Areas where the aeration is higher also seem to be preferred. The eggs can be transferred to a small (2 1/2-gallon) tank with a sponge filter (this is done with many species of *Corydoras* for initial raising). Anywhere from 30 to more than 100 large yellowish eggs may be laid by two pairs of

Another species with a similar color pattern is Corydoras simulatus. *A comparison of the photos on these two pages will help distinguish these species. Photo: H.-J. Richter.*

spawners. They hatch in about four or five days at 24° to 25°C. The fry can be raised easily with a starting food of microworms and newly hatched brine shrimp as soon as the yolk sac disappears. The newly hatched fry are tan with some speckling and the beginnings of a mask through the eyes. After about three weeks the dorsal fin starts frequently be seen off the bottom browsing on plants (both the upper and lower sides of the leaves). In a well planted aquarium that had some flowerpots added, *C. elegans* exhibited some territorial behavior by taking possession of the pots and became somewhat aggressive. Battles between males were of greater and

Corydoras nanus (or a closely related form). This species pattern is very similar to that of C. elegans *seen on the opposite page. Photo: K. Paysan.*

to become darker and at five weeks the dark band on the back makes its appearance. By the time the young reach a length of 2 cm or so most of the speckling disappears and they look like their parents. The spawning itself lasts a few hours at a time but may be continued over a period of a couple of days. They may be ready to spawn again in about two weeks if they are properly conditioned.

Corydoras elegans comes from sluggish creeks with clear, alkaline water of the middle Amazon. It attains a length of about 6 cm. Although not a midwater species like *C. hastatus* and *C. pygmaeus, elegans* can greater violence as the female filled up with eggs. Males were said to clean the undersides of some of the leaves. When the female started to similarly clean, the males became very active in trying to force their attentions on her and crowd out the other males. Eventually spawning occurred and continued about every fourth day over a seven-week period. Although most reports of this species's spawning say it agrees with the basic behavior of the *Corydoras* spawning (including the "T" position), one aquarist said his *elegans* never did assume the "T" position. The actual spawning occurred a short distance above

Corydoras elegans *can be territorial and aggressive, especially when ripe females are near. The underside of leaves are the preferred sites for depositing eggs. Photo: H.-J. Richter.*

the bottom and the spawners slowly sank to the bottom, after which the female left to deposit the eggs she laid. The eggs are fairly small, about 1.2 mm in diameter, and yellowish in color, although they turn darker as they develop. They are placed mainly on the underside of plant leaves *(Cryptocoryne* were used in one report), but also were found on the glass sides of the aquarium and on the plant roots. At about 26°C the fry hatch out in three or four days. Some 8 to 25 eggs were spawned during each bout,

Corydoras elegans *originates in sluggish creeks where the pH is on the alkaline side. It attains a length of about 6cm. Photo: B. Kahl.*

Corydoras griseus *is almost devoid of any pattern. It has not gained much favor in the aquarium world. Photo: Heiko Bleher.*

and a total per spawning of more than 350 eggs was counted. The newly hatched fry look like the fry of *C. hastatus*, but at about 12 mm a dark horizontal stripe makes its appearance along with a spot in the dorsal fin. The stripe disappears later and a series of bands appears. Early foods should be microworms and newly hatched brine shrimp along with cultured rotifers if available. With good feeding the *elegans* can reach sexual maturity in about ten months.

Corydoras cochui was

Corydoras *sp. allied to* C. latus. *Not much is known about this species and because of its drab coloration it has not become popular. Photo: H.-J. Richter.*

Two variations of Corydoras nanus. *This colorful species is gaining in popularity and should eventually be in good supply.*

originally collected in the Rio Araguaia, Goiaz, Brazil. It is a small species of less than 4 cm and as such requires smaller food particles than those fed to the larger *Corydoras* species. It is largely transparent but with dark spots in a row on the side and some small dark spots on the head and back. The dorsal and caudal also have dark spots. A golden sheen is seen when the body is lighted in a certain way, making it an attractive species. Spawning is standard, with the eggs being placed mostly on

Corydoras undulatus *showing two variations in color pattern. The above individual has less solid body color and more of a pattern on the caudal base. Photo: Dr. Warren E. Burgess (above); H.-J. Richter (below).*

leaves of plants, in one instance *Sagittaria* being the preferred spot. The eggs hatched in about four days, with the fry burrowing into the bottom gravel as they dropped to the bottom.

Corydoras undulatus comes from northern Argentina and southeastern Brazil. It attains a length of about 5.5 cm. It spawns in a method similar to that of *C. aeneus,* possibly precipitated by a water change with water slightly

cooler than that removed. The small, clear eggs are usually deposited on the underside of plant leaves, usually in clusters of 25 to 50 eggs per leaf.

Corydoras habrosus is a small (less than 4 cm) species from Venezuela. It tends to school somewhat more than *C. aeneus* or *C. paleatus.* It is easy to spawn, and the spawning behavior resembles that of *C. aeneus.* Spawning usually occurs

Corydoras habrosus. *Photo: H.-J. Richter.*

Corydoras leucomelas. *Photo: Dr. Herbert R. Axelrod.*

Corydoras semiaquilus. *Photo: Dr. Herbert R. Axelrod.*

Corydoras ambiacus *(above) is commonly confused with* C. agassizi *and perhaps* C. pulcher. C. robinae *(below) has a very distinctive caudal fin pattern similar to that of* Dianema urostriatum. *It is currently being called the Flagtail Cory. Photos: K. Paysan (above); Dr. Warren E. Burgess (below).*

in the morning hours, resulting in a number of egg clusters made up of about 25 to 40 eggs adhering to the glass, filter boxes and stems, or whatever is available. These are ignored (usually) by the parents and hatch in about five to seven days. The fry drop to the bottom and immediately hide. On about the second day the fry can be fed

microworms and baby brine shrimp. The fry are said to be sensitive to water conditions, so a little extra care in keeping the water clean and in making water changes must be exercised.

Corydoras adolfoi is a moderate-sized *Corydoras* from the upper Rio Negro attaining a length of about 6 cm. This species breeds very much like *C.*

aeneus. A successful spawning has been initiated by a water change using water two to three degrees cooler than that which had been removed, in concordance with a greater turbulence of the water created by a power filter. The males (in about a 2 to 1 ratio to females) began their courtship by a frenzied chasing of the females. The males were usually above and behind and to one side or the other, and would touch the female on the top of the head. Although most of the males

from the water's surface. Only a single egg at a time was deposited (actually on rare occasions two eggs might be laid at one time). The eggs, about 25% smaller than those of *C. aeneus,* were a milky white or pearly white with a dark spot; infertile eggs became a dead white and were readily attacked by fungus. Once the eggs were placed there was a resting period of a couple of minutes duration, after which the males suddenly (by some signal?) took interest in her again. Over a period of four

Corydoras adolfoi *(shown here) and* C. robinae *(opposite page) are two species of* Corydoras *recently described in* T.F.H. *magazine. Notice the golden spot behind the eyeband. Photo: Dr. Herbert R. Axelrod.*

would join in the chasing of the females, only one or two would be the main "suitors." The usual "T" position was assumed for five to ten seconds, after which there was a short 10 to 12 second rest. The female would clean the spot just before the deposition of the eggs after some two to eight minutes elapsed while she searched for just the right one. Most of the time this would be in the upper 12 mm of the water, the rest rarely below about 5 cm

to eight hours 22-46 eggs were laid. The parents took no notice of the eggs once spawning was completed, perhaps because they were at such a high level. By the third day the eyes were visible in the eggs, and by the fifth day they started to hatch. The last of the eggs hatched more than 24 hours later. It took about three days for the yolk to be absorbed and the raising could proceed like that of *C. aeneus.*

A sequence in the courtship and spawning of Corydoras adolfoi. *Photos: G. Hickson.*

Corydoras guapore *(above) and* C. panda *(below) are members of the complex of species characterized by a dark spot on or near the caudal base. Photos: H.-J. Richter.*

Corydoras panda is a moderately small (4.5-5 cm) species from the Rio Ucayali system. It was recently collected live from Rio Lullapichis, a tributary of Rio Pachitea, in a clear mountain stream with a rocky bottom. In the area where *C. panda* was taken the trees closed in overhead to form a canopy so that the sun could shine only in scattered places and only for a short time. The water itself had a temperature range of about 22° to 23.5°C although it could vary between 21° and 28°C. The carbonate hardness (total) was 3.1° and the pH 7.7. No water plants and no mulm were present except in small still-water pockets. The water moved freely in the dry season when the specimens were captured but was expected to be a torrential stream in the rainy season, a rather unusual

Corydoras caudomaculatus. *Photo: H.-J. Richter.*

Corydoras guapore. *Photo: Heiko Bleher.*

Corydoras steindachneri. *Photo: D. Sands.*

107

habitat for *Corydoras*. The individuals captured were about 3.5 to 4 cm long, sand colored, and had black markings across the eyes, in the dorsal fin, and at the caudal peduncle.

In captivity *C. panda* was spawned in a 30-liter tank with no bottom cover but with an inside filter, Java moss, and some hiding places formed from clay bowls or flowerpots. On a diet that included daphnia, tubificid worms, chironomid larvae, and even frozen foods, they grew to nearly 5 cm. There was a water change of 33% every two days. The water had a total hardness of 10°, a carbonate hardness of 13°, and the temperature was 22° to 24°C. *C. panda* seems to propagate better in small groups during a particular season. They would spawn mainly from December to April, which coincided with the rainy season in their natural habitat. The sexes are difficult to distinguish outside the spawning season as the female does not get very robust. Spawning proceeded in normal *Corydoras* fashion. The eggs were about 1.5 mm in diameter, clear, and with a yellow-gold color. They became light brown after three days and dark brown after four days when the eyes became visible. About 12 hours later the eggs hatched. The fry were 7.5 mm in length and possessed a yolk sac that was absorbed in another day and a half. At that time they accepted baby brine shrimp and microworms. In another ten days the fry grew to 11 mm and were given in addition to the other food some chopped grindal worms.

The color pattern started as pigmentation in the area of the forehead, nape, and behind the gill covers. A few days after hatching these areas became darker and at one week the dorsal and caudal fins began to differentiate from the embryonic fin membranes. By two weeks the dark pigment around the eyes was distinctly darker and dark markings seen at the front and back of the dorsal fin and on the caudal peduncle intensified. By the end of four weeks the fry were 2 cm long and resembled

Corydoras ambiacus is commonly available and readily spawned in captivity making it a desirable species. Photo: H.-.Richter.

Corydoras haraldschultzi *is an attractive cory with many horizontal stripes on the body as compared to* ambiacus *and other species with only a few. Photo: H. Mayland.*

the adults; the dark pigment behind the gill covers was almost gone at this time.

After about a month the adults spawned again, and this continued at intervals of four to 24 days over the breeding season. The number of eggs fluctuated from a low of 18 to a high of over 60 in the dozen spawnings obtained. The eggs were rarely attached to the glass sides of the tank but most usually to the Java moss with some of them scattered on the bottom. The newly hatched pandas seem to be sensitive to disturbances.

Corydoras barbatus is a relatively large species attaining a length of over 10 cm. It is quite common in almost all bodies of water along the Sao Paulo coast from Santos to Rio de Janeiro, but more likely to be found in soft and quite acid (pH 5 or lower) tea-colored (black-water) streams where the water is clear and flowing briskly over sand or sand with pebbles and scattered rock slabs bottoms. These areas are subject to winter flooding. The temperatures are relatively cool, not rising much above 20°C in the summertime and dropping to perhaps 10° to 12°C in the wintertime for short periods. *C. barbatus* has been found together with *C. nattereri* and *C. macropterus. C. barbatus* is a bottom-dweller commonly found in groups of up to 50 or more along the sides of the rivers or creeks, where they can quickly disappear under the dense shrubbery. It has the ability to change the pattern somewhat depending upon the bottom type, and it has been said that the Rio populations differ somewhat from those collected about Santos. The slightly larger females were also captured among some flooded channels away from the creek during flood tide; few adult males were present.

Sexes are easily distinguishable. They not only differ in color (the males being much more colorful), but the males have their cheeks covered by bristles (these are weak or absent in females) and their

109

Corydoras barbatus. *The male is seen in the top photo, the female in the center photo, and a front view of the male's head in the lower photo. Photos:*

pectoral spines are more developed. In addition, the first two rays of the dorsal fin are more elongate in the male. At a length of about 7 cm the males were readily identifiable, even though their cheek bristles had not yet made their appearance.

Suggested tank setups include a layer of fine sand (*barbatus* are said to like to burrow, sometimes becoming almost completely covered), some rocks. Plants are optional, and one breeder added spawning mops for receiving the eggs. A variety of live and dried foods were sufficient to keep the fish in good condition. The temperature range should be from about 20° to 25°C, although this species is reported to have spawned at 18° C in the wild. Apparently the parents will spawn under a variety of water conditions — up to pH 7.2 and a temperature of

26°C — but in their natural habitat the pH is less than 5 and the temperature is closer to 18° so these conditions should be approached if a successful spawn is desired. It has been reported that the acid condition is a prerequisite for a good hatch. An inside filter with peat moss has been suggested for bringing the pH down to proper levels. In addition, the spawners should have as much peace and quiet as possible. With heavy feedings of tubificid worms and other live foods spawning should occur.

When things get going the female seems to be the aggressor; sometimes when nudging the male on his side she will push him all the way across the tank and pin him against the glass wall of the tank. The "T" position is held for several seconds and may occur both in midwater and on the bottom.

A male Corydoras barbatus *with the spectacular head and anterior body pattern. Photo: B. Frank.*

Top view of male Corydoras barbatus *showing the light streak from snout to dorsal interrupting the color pattern, as well as bristles along the side of the head. Photo: B. Frank.*

About three to six eggs are laid, and as the male rests on the bottom the female searches for a place to put the eggs. There does not seem to be a pattern in the distribution of the eggs, but they are usually near the surface. About half a dozen are in a cluster and as many as 130 have been reported for a single spawn. Spawning lasts for half an hour to an hour. The eggs are approximately 1.7 mm in diameter and hatch out in about three or four days. After another two days the fry have absorbed the yolk sac and will accept microworms and newly hatched brine shrimp. At this time they are about 3 mm long. The fry grow quickly if properly fed, and in a month and a half they are about 18 mm long. Spawnings occurred at about weekly intervals. If the pH rose considerably the percentage of eggs that hatched decreased significantly.

Corydoras macropterus is from the same area but does not attain the large size of *C. barbatus,* the average size being about 6 cm. It is not encountered in the usual coastal waters but prefers small brooks or creeks that are shaded by overhanging trees. The water is tea-colored and the bottom covered with decaying leaves; the banks are muddy. Underwater plants are scarce but fallen branches and twigs are plentiful. The *C. macropterus* are seen more often lying on a horizontal branch or leaf in midwater like *C. hastatus.* Like *C. barbatus, C. macropterus* males have bristles on the cheek. They have extremely elongate dorsal and pectoral fin spines as well, more developed than in any other *Corydoras* species. The two sexes are about the same size. *C. macropterus* is considered a peaceful species that will accept the usual foods that it grubs from the bottom substrate in the normal fashion.

Very little need be said about other species that are commonly imported from South America, as they act and breed much like the species already discussed, especially *C. aeneus* and *C. paleatus*. *C. arcuatus* is reported a little harder to spawn (try softer water); *C. rabauti* may yield as many as 800 eggs per spawn that hatch in five to eight days; *C. garbei* spawns no more than about 20 large (2.5 mm in diameter) eggs; *C. undulatus* is said to be sexually dichromatic; *C. zygatus* has eggs that are 1.5

The spectacular Corydoras macropterus. *The upper photo shows a male with the extremely elongate dorsal and pectoral fin spines; the lower photo shows the female. Photos: K. Paysan.*

C. rabauti, *4-6 weeks old.*

C. rabauti, *3 months old.*

C. rabauti *(left) and* C. zygatus *(right) compared side by side. Photos: I. Fuller.*

C. zygatus. *4 weeks old.*

C. zygatus, *3 months old.*

A side by side pair of Corydoras arcuatus. *The arcuate band along the back gave it the specific name.*

mm in diameter but the female can lay up to 400 eggs per spawning; *C. melanistius brevirostris* is said to be sensitive to fresh tap water; and *C. nattereri*, a lover of cooler water, shows symptoms of distress at temperatures above 24°C. *Corydoras rabauti* prefers the upper range of temperatures (24°-28°C) and cannot tolerate low temperatures. It is actually sensitive to temperature fluctuations as well. Spawning reports (sometimes as *C. myersi*, a synonym) indicate the young are quite distinctly colored at first. Up to a length of about 12 mm the front half of the body is green and the back half a reddish color.

Corydoras narcissus *looks quite different from* arcuatus *but note the dark line in approximately the same position. Photo: Dr. Herbert R. Axelrod.*

Corydoras garbei *spawns no more than about 20 large eggs compared with as many as 800 for* C. rabauti. *Photo: Dr. Herbert R. Axelrod.*

C. reticulatus has an unusual history. Fraser-Brunner's specimens were aquarium fish (a pair) that were loaned to a German aquarist for breeding purposes and were not preserved. Fraser-Brunner redescribed the species (1947) based on a specimen from "Monte Alegre, River Amazon"

that Weitzman (1960) designated as a neotype while re-redescribing the species. Incidentally, when keeping this species fresh tap water and. highly acid water should be avoided.

The resemblance of the Callichthyidae to the Loricariidae is quite basic and includes such

Corydoras robustus *is one of those species only rarely seen. Some species are only found mixed with regularly imported species by sharp-eyed aquarists. Photo: Dr. Herbert R. Axelrod.*

Corydoras melanistius brevirostris is one of the few subspecies described in this large genus.

things as the armor, the structure of the cranium and of the labyrinth system, and the structure of the vertebrae. They do differ, however, by the participation of the skull in the anterior closure of the capsule (Chardon, 1968). The Callichthyidae also seem to be allied to the Astroblepidae, the Trichomycteridae, and the Aspredinidae (Chardon, 1968).

These five families have in common the following characters: the unpaired sinus is not separated from the medulla oblongata by any processes of the exoccipital; the anterior points of the sacculae are vestigial or missing; and the lagenas are abnormally dorsal (Chardon, 1968). They of course share other characters that are also shared by other catfish families.

Corydoras reticulatus variety. It is always interesting to search through a tankful of C. reticulatus *to see how many different color patterns can be seen. Photo: Andre Roth.*

Beautifully decorated, this aquarium not only looks good but also makes the needs of the fishes it will house its major consideration. Many different hiding places have been provided, yet plenty of free swimming area has been left. Photo courtesy Penn-Plax, Inc.

Bibliography

Chardon, M. 1968. "Anatomie comparée de l'appareil de Weber et des structures connexes chez les Siluriformes," *Ann. Mus. Roy. Afr. Centr.,* sér. VIII, Sci. Zool., 169:1-285.

Fraser-Brunner, A. 1947. "New fishes of the genus *Corydoras,"* *Proc. Zool. Soc. (London),* 117(1):241-246.

Gosline, W. A. 1940. "A revision of the Neotropical catfishes of the family Callichthyidae," *Stanford Ichth. Bull.,* 2(1):1-29.

Hoedeman, J. 1974. *Naturalists' Guide to Fresh-Water Aquarium Fish.* Sterling Publ. Co., Inc., New York. 1152 pp.

Miranda-Ribeiro, P. de. 1959. "Catálogo dos peixes do Museu Nacional, 3. Callichthyidae Gill, 1872, *Publições. avuls. Mus. nac. Rio de Janeiro,* 27:1-16.

Myers, G. S. 1953. "A note on the habits and classification of *Corydoras hastatus,"* *Aquarium Journal* (San Francisco), 24(11):268-270.

Nijssen, H. 1970. "Revision of the Surinam catfishes of the genus *Corydoras* Lacépède, 1803 (Pisces, Siluriformes, Callichthyidae)," *Beaufortia,* 18(230):1-75.

Nijssen, H. & I. Isbrücker, 1970. "The South American catfish genus *Brochis* Cope, 1872 (Pisces, Siluriformes, Callichthyidae)," *Beaufortia,* 18(236):151-168.

———,1980. "A review of the genus *Corydoras* Lacépède, 1803 (Pisces, Siluriformes, Callichthyidae)," *Bijd. tot de Dierk.,* 50(1):190-220.

Weitzman, S. H. 1960. "Figures and description of a South American catfish, *Corydoras reticulatus* Fraser-Brunner," *Stanford Ichth. Bull.,* 7(4):155-161.

Index

A COMPLETE INTRODUCTION TO

CORYDORAS

and Related Catfishes

CO-015

Corydoras catfishes and kids go together—chances are that young children will see more of *Corydoras* species than most other fishes in a community aquarium, because the corys stay mostly at the bottom of the tank, more or less on a level with young children's eyes. Photo by Dr. Herbert R. Axelrod.

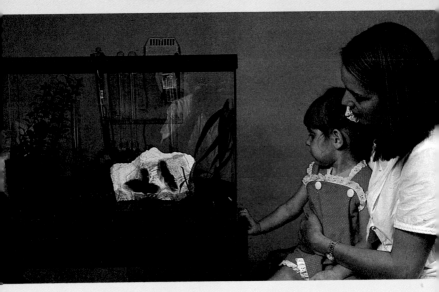